GOD PUT A
FIGHTER IN ME

GOD PUT A FIGHTER IN ME

Sheila Walsh

HODDER AND STOUGHTON
LONDON   SYDNEY   AUCKLAND   TORONTO

British Library Cataloguing in Publication Data

Walsh, Sheila
  God put a fighter in me.
  1. Christian life
  I. Title
  248.4   BV4501.2

ISBN 0 340 39212 6

This book is dedicated to two ladies who have recently gone to be with the Lord:

Joan Hearn – her constant love and friendship made America feel like home.
Maureen Martin – whose life spoke volumes about the Kingdom of God.

I wish to thank the following people:

Gill Snow, who by divine inspiration managed to decipher my handwriting and faithfully type the manuscript!

Cliff Richard, who has been such a wonderful friend to Norman and me.

Bill Latham, for his encouragement, bribes and threats!

Gerald and Anona Coates, who share our lives, our hopes and dreams, and the mortgage!

Gilbert and Connie Kirby, the youngest couple I know.

My family, who have supported me in so many ways – especially you, Mum. Thank you for trusting God in me and making it possible for me to follow my heart.

Lastly, never least, *Norman*. You are the best friend a girl could ever have. I love you.

CONTENTS

(The chapter titles are taken from the titles of some of Sheila Walsh's recent songs.)

INTRODUCTION

When I was asked if I'd like to write a book, it seemed an awesome task. Where do you begin to write all the things that are on your heart and about the people who have touched your life? As I looked back at all the ingredients, from Scotland to India, London Bible College to Las Vegas, Billy Graham to Cliff Richard, I picked up my pen, looked at an empty notepad and sighed!

I've had so much fun. I've laughed again at stupid mistakes I've made. I've cried a few more tears at things that changed my life irrevocably, and I've realised afresh what a wonderful God we serve. My life has been made so much richer because of the people who have crossed my path. I hope that somehow, in that divine intangible way, your life will be touched too.

1

GROWING UP TO BE A CHILD

'If I don't do it now, it'll never be done.' My mother, Elizabeth, was down on her knees planting lettuces. A few hours later I was brought into the world by a young midwife in my parents' bedroom. I was born in a mining town in Scotland called Cumnock, in 1956.

We had a lovely house with a large garden. At the bottom of the garden stood a beautiful Catholic church, set in its own grounds. The priest's housekeeper was a very friendly lady. She would take my elder sister and me in to watch special services from the church balcony. My favourite was always when the little girls came to take their first communion, looking like pretty brides in long white dresses. It seemed such a shame to me that our Baptist church didn't insist on such finery.

Looking back on our childhood, it's difficult to distinguish between what we actually remember ourselves and what we've heard our families smiling about over cups of tea in nostalgic moments.

My sister, Frances, was a very good little girl. She would sit for hours with one toy, playing very happily and never getting dirty. Unfortunately, I was not the dainty type. I felt that life was one large sea of adventure, and I wanted to jump in. If I hadn't climbed several trees, made friends with a new dog, ripped my dress, and caught some new little beastie to keep in a box, it was a remarkably quiet morning!

My father was a very tall, warm-hearted man, with a wonderful voice. He would often appear home with the strangest collection of people who needed help. He shared the reality of his relationship with God in a very tangible way. To a little girl, these tramps and vagabonds were an exciting new breed, with all sorts of stories. My mum would run a nice hot bath for them, provide them with a meal and food for the road. They would leave us, smelling marginally sweeter and, hopefully, less hungry. After they had left, our bathroom always seemed to resemble a rabbit hutch, with straw and hay strewn everywhere.

When I was almost three years old, my mum told us that she was going to have another baby. We all really hoped for a little boy to complete our family. Just before Christmas, he arrived. He was the lovliest thing I'd ever seen, we called him Stephen.

It seemed to me that the only thing we didn't have was a dog. I begged and begged to have a puppy. I promised that I'd brush his coat and share my dinner with him – all sorts of supposedly persuasive entreaties. One evening, I was all tucked up in bed, waiting for my dad to read me a story. He came in with his hands behind his back and told me to close my eyes and hold out my hands. All of a sudden, I was aware that some living creature had just crawled up the sleeve of my pyjamas. After a lot of yelling and running round the room like an idiot, I discovered that it was a little dachshund puppy. Her name was Heidi. She was a very highly strung dog, with interesting peculiarities. My favourite one was that every time someone rang the door bell she wet the carpet!

My parents were very committed Christians, and we all attended our local Baptist church. My mum had been a very keen believer since she was a child and her faith was certainly put to the test. One night, as we all lay asleep, a blood clot moved into my father's brain and when he awoke he was paralysed down one side and had lost the power of speech. He was taken off to hospital and spent a long time on the critical list. When he came home, he still couldn't speak, but he could walk with the aid of a stick. We had a speech therapist who came to the house and tried to help Dad, but it just didn't work. It was a terribly difficult time. My little baby brother became very ill with pneumonia while Dad was in hospital, and Mum spent all her time dashing between the two wards. Frances and I were taken care of by kind neighbours who wanted to help in any way they could. We had to sell Heidi, as she was an added burden for my mum.

After a few months my father's condition deteriorated and at times he would become quite violent as a brainstorm would rack his body. He was eventually taken away and he died shortly afterwards.

My mum decided that it would be good if we returned to the town where she was born, so we packed up and moved to Ayr. We found a smaller house, with a little garden, and settled in. I have very few memories of the first years after my father's death. It seemed a colourless time.

My little brother recovered from his pneumonia and he was a joy to us all. He and I were great friends as we were growing up – I loved to play football, rugby and all the rough games that boys enjoyed. We also used to play hopscotch, drawing out boxes on the road with chalk and playing with a large piece of marble, sending it into the different squares. One day Stephen picked up the marble and decided to throw it across the street just as I walked past. It hit me right in the eye and, as I ran in to tell my mum that disaster had struck, I fell over a chair and hit the other eye on a piece of furniture. We must have looked a strange family that Sunday, as we walked to church with Stephen laughing his head off at my two black eyes!

I took to school like a duck to water. I enjoyed making new friends and did well at my work. For the first few years

I was either first or second in my class, which was a great
delight to my gran. My mum's mum was a wonderful
woman, with a unique sense of humour. I know now that
she suffered a lot, as she had bad asthma, but
she never ever complained. She came to visit us every
Thursday and it was always the highlight of my week. The
only thing that tormented me at this time were the terrible
nightmares I used to have about my father. Every night it
was the same: I would dream that he was coming to get me,
because I had pushed his stick away and made him fall.
Many mornings I would wake up weeping into my pillow. I
walked in my sleep most nights, so Mum had a gate put up
at the top of the stairs so that I wouldn't fall down.

We had moved again to another house, as the town
authorities wanted to build where we were living. I found
my new school very strange. I guess in many ways it was
my first taste of how cruel children can be to each other. We
had a very fat boy in our class and he was tormented
constantly by the other boys. One girl seemed to think it
was funny that my father had died and taunted me about it
continuously. From being a very outgoing friendly little
girl, I became much more withdrawn and introspective. I
hated to let my mother out of my sight. I can remember
when my gran suggested that my mum needed a break and
she wanted them to go away for a week together. Frances,
Stephen and I went to stay with my aunt and uncle. They
are such a lovely couple, but it was a miserable week for me.
I was sure that I would never see my mum again.

I grew up with a very strong picture of God as part of our
family. It made a deep impression on me to see that my
mum still believed in a loving God despite her personal
tragedy. Her faith was strong and practical. Financially
these were very difficult years, with our income being
restricted to a widow's pension. Mum believed totally that
the Lord would provide for us. We prayed for everything
we needed. I remember on one occasion Stephen needed

new trousers and we simply didn't have enough money to buy them, so we prayed. I remember wondering why God would keep a supply of spare trousers in heaven! It seems He does, because they arrived the next day, via a kind lady in our church. My mum never became bitter or angry at God, and her faith was a constant source of strength to us all.

When I was eleven years old, a gospel group from Edinburgh called 'The Heralds' came to town. They held a crusade in our local cinema and we all went along. That night, as the evangelist, Ian Leitch, spoke about the Lord Jesus, God spoke to me. He made it so clear that one doesn't 'inherit' Christianity. Ian said that God has no grand-children, only sons and daughters. That evening many people went forward to accept Jesus, but I felt my legs would never get me to the front. The next evening, in the quiet of my own bedroom, my mum prayed with me and I became part of God's family. Although I was young, I knew with all my heart that this was real.

It's amazing how old you feel at twelve, when you get your new uniform and move up to senior school. I was so excited that I was up and dressed by half past six! My new school was situated right next to a large Catholic school. My uniform was a very smart navy and gold blazer, and a grey skirt that was about as exciting as a weekend in Margate! I caught the bus to school, hopped off and went in. I was inside the gates for a full five minutes before I noticed that everyone else had green blazers on and I was in the wrong place!

I spent six years at Mainholm Academy and generally had a great time. My music teacher was a really lovely lady who showed a lot of interest in me. I had never thought of myself as a singer before, but she trained me up for the lead part in the school's Christmas musical. Unfortunately, it was *West Side Story* that year. I found it very difficult at thirteen years of age, with spots and white socks, to sing 'I

Feel Pretty' with any real conviction! The following year she put me in for two classes in a music festival. I was so nervous, and consumed fourteen packets of mentholyptus tablets before I went on. The adjudicator was very kind. He said that he felt I had talent, but if I could learn to sing in tune as well it would help!

My life at this stage was very definitely split down the middle. At school I had one set of friends, and at church a totally different crowd. My best friend at church was a girl called Andree. We were totally different in background, but I admired her tremendously. Neither of her parents were Christians, and yet she radiated the life and love of Jesus. She taught me so much about sharing your faith in a real, natural way. We had a great youth group and on Saturday evenings we opened a club at church that we could invite kids off the street into. God blessed our unprofessional efforts tremendously and we saw so many people saved. We bombarded the town with tracts, 'Jesus stickers' and free Bibles – no-one was safe. I remember sitting on a bus one day, when a poor unsuspecting man came and sat beside me. He pulled out a packet of cigarettes, removed one and asked me if I had a light. I said, 'No, but I have the Light of the World.' He looked at me for a few seconds, wondering if I was dangerous, and then slipped quietly away!

As Mum was missionary secretary in our church, I met a healthy supply of missionaries. They would often come home with us for lunch and their talk of life in the bush fascinated me. I had visions of myself, hacking my way through the dark mysterious undergrowth, with gospels in my rucksack. I began to read the life stories of the more famous of these pioneers. Hudson Taylor's story was riveting. I read of his cry to God to give him China and a great idea occurred. I decided to begin on home soil. That day, after school, I went down to the beach and stood by the water's edge. In as loud and authoritative voice as I could muster, I yelled, 'God, give me Scotland!' Unfortunately, as the tide was just turning, all I got was wet feet!

As my interest in music grew, my mum decided that it would be good if I went to private singing lessons. She found me a wonderful old teacher called Mr Tweddle. At my first lesson he asked me to sing a favourite song, and he sat back and listened. After I finished, there was a pregnant pause, before he told me that he thought I sounded like a cross between a sheep and a machine gun! He was a real perfectionist! He made me stand up against the music room wall and sing the most ridiculous assortment of phrases. After a few months of harrowing training, he put me in for the same two classes in the music festival. When I was placed first in both, I threw my arms around his neck and kissed his bald head! He was very keen that I should train to be an opera singer. My only concern was that all the ones that I'd seen seemed to weigh about 200 pounds!

A few days after the competitions, I received a call from a young Christian music teacher. He told me that he was the musical director for a gospel group, and would I be interested in joining? I didn't know that we had any British gospel music, so I was intrigued. I went along to a practice and met the members of Unity. There were about fourteen of them. I liked their music a lot and happily joined them. The first few weeks were simply practices in someone's home, and then the first concert arrived. I had been given a solo to sing, but I had never used a microphone before. Mr Tweddle had taught me to project my voice to the back of a hall, unaided by modern electronics! When my spot arrived, I picked up the mike and belted forth with great gusto. I'm led to believe that several dogs in the neighbourhood were laid to rest that night with perforated eardrums! As we sang, mostly in churches, we wore long pink gingham dresses and looked like a cross between Tammy Wynette and Little Bo Peep!

For two years we travelled all over Scotland at weekends and during school holidays, singing and speaking about our faith. One evening, Raymond, our drummer, suggested that I should speak at the end of the concert and give an altar call. I was petrified, and convinced that I would dry up in the middle and stand there looking like the worst advertisement for Christianity that you've ever seen. I locked myself in the toilet for an hour before the concert and prayed for words to say. I only spoke for about fifteen minutes, but that evening fourteen young people gave their lives to God. I was ecstatic; I didn't sleep all night. I marched round and round my bedroom, singing choruses at the top of my voice, much to the disgust of my sister, who was trying to sleep!

I came to a point where I decided it was all or nothing. Either God is God and, if He is, He deserves everything; or it's all false and merits nothing. I knew it had to be all. I went to see Mr Tweddle and told him that I'd decided not to be an opera singer, but I was going to be a missionary instead. In my mind, I'd settled on India – fewer spiders and snakes. I applied to study at London Bible College and was accepted.

The last few weeks before I went were so difficult. I'd never been away from home before, and I was leaving behind all my friends and family. I packed up my favourite belongings, said goodbye to Mum, and got on the train to London. As I sat, with tears dripping off my chin, I wondered what lay ahead of me.

2

FUTURE EYES

As the train hurried past fields and houses, I began to cheer up a little. I knew that I wasn't on my own – God was with me. I'd never before been in a situation where it was just me and the Lord. It was exciting – even the British Rail sandwiches couldn't dampen my enthusiasm!

A few hours later we pulled into Euston Station in London. Everyone rushed to get off, and I sat for a few moments, wondering how I would get my three suitcases, a sleeping-bag, and a Snoopy dog off the train. A friend of our family, who lived in London, had offered to meet me, which was just as well, as I'm sure that otherwise I'd still be sitting on Platform 5!

We took the tube and then a train to a very quaint scenic village called Chorleywood, where I would be staying with a widowed lady. She lived in a beautiful little cottage called 'Coppelia' on the edge of a forest. Nina made me feel so at home in my first few weeks. She worked with a missionary organisation and often went away to Germany for extended periods of time, leaving me the run of her house and her pussy-cat.

The first few weeks at London Bible College were a blur of new faces, books, coffee parties, books, lectures, books and more books! I soon discovered that a girl on the same course as mine lived next door to me. Marion was quite a character. She always wore a black cape, hail or shine, had a

degree in Zoology, a car that only started about one morning in six, and an unhealthy preoccupation with rats,
snakes and other slimy beasts.

Our course was quite intensive, and we were advised to
study for three hours a night. All I can say is that I was not a
natural. I preferred the more practical side of things and
joined about forty-three prayer groups! I eventually had to
cut back a bit, as I kept getting mixed up and praying for the
wrong thing in the wrong place. Somehow praying for
Africa in the pro-life prayer group seemed a shade 'out on a
limb'.

The course was varied and interesting. We studied everything from philosophy to Church history, Greek to ethics. I
particularly enjoyed the Old Testament studies. It was as if
a whole new world was opened up to me. Somehow,
knowing the historical, social and economic situation in
Israel cast such light on books that before seemed dry and,
at times, even irrelevant. My awareness of God as a patient
merciful Father was heightened immeasurably. It was
wonderful to read of how the Lord hates injustice and
cruelty, how He defends the weak and hopeless. How
God's heart must have ached for His people as He consist-
ently showered them with love and grace, and incessantly
they turned away from Him.

The principal at London Bible College in my time was a
wonderful man called Gilbert Kirby. He and his wife,
Connie, had loving pastoral hearts towards the student
body. I remember my first encounter with them so well.
All the new students were invited to visit them in their
home, in alphabetical order. The day of the Ws arrived
and, as usual, I was in the wrong place at the wrong
time. I suddenly realised that it was 1 p.m. and I was
supposed to be there by then. I ran all the way and, as
the door was open, I knocked, went in, fell over the
golden retriever puppy, and landed nose down on the
carpet! I was told afterwards that it helped to break

the ice, but I was more concerned with a potential broken nose!

The College encouraged all students to live on campus in their final year of study. I think the theory was that, if one is closer to the library, study will come more easily. All I can say is that you can drag a horse to water but you can't make it drink! I've always been hopeless at consistent study; life seems far too short to bury my head in A4 paper!

I was one of the youngest girls on my course, being only nineteen. Many of the girls taking the Diploma in Theology were in their mid-thirties and from fairly conservative backgrounds. The College had become more flexible about dress codes, allowing girls to wear trousers to class – further evidence to me that we serve a merciful God!

When I'd gone to Edinburgh with my friend Andree for a day during a College holiday, I had purchased a new coat. 'Coat' is perhaps a generous name for it; it was more like a Afghan dog. When I bought it, it was a lovely sunny day, but unfortunately when it rained the coat smelled fairly strongly of dead animal. One day, back in London, I headed off in a heavy shower to buy a new notepad. I returned to the library, hung my coat over a chair, and went to scan the shelves for a book on situation ethics. I became aware of a terrible scuffle at the far end of the library. I had, it seemed, been followed back by a large hairy canine creature, who was now attempting to get better acquainted with my coat in a corner!

I love boots. I have always loved boots. I bought a pair of lovely red leather ones from a friend's shoe shop, unaware of the controversy they would provoke. One lovely Spring day I was lying on the grass under a tree, trying not to think of what I should be doing, when three figures came be-tween me and the sunshine. I sat up, to see some of the girls from my course who had obviously come to speak to me. They sat down, and one of the more outspoken girls launched in. In a gentle voice she explained that several of them felt I was a stumbling-block. Surely no spiritual girl would wear Levis and could I imagine Gladys Aylward wearing red leather boots. My first thought was, 'I can't imagine her wearing your stupid woolly hat either,' but I quickly repented! I tried to explain how I saw things, but it simply didn't communicate well. I felt sad and so alone. Was I really ungodly? How could boots be non-Christian and knitted twin-sets Christian? I really wanted to please God, but the thought of going around for the rest of my life looking like an extra from *Little House on the Prairie* didn't appeal either! I decided that I'd had enough of College, that I didn't fit in anywhere, and I would leave. I made an appointment to go and see Mr Kirby. He's such a kind man; he sat me down and just listened. I ranted and raved about endless hours spent studying while the world went to ruin. I told him nobody liked me, I hated Greek, tweed skirts, and College lunches! I thought he'd blow up at me and throw me out, but he really did the opposite. He told me that he was sure I was learning more than I realised, that God is not in a hurry, and that He loves me as I am. He made me understand one of the great joys of the Christian life – God does not squeeze us into ill-fitting moulds, turning us all out alike. God works in our hearts, refining us and making us more like His Son, but He never crushes our personality. His family is like a beautiful tapestry, with room for us all.

I'm sure it's very therapeutic to mix with people from all sorts of different Churches, countries and cultures.

I had been brought up in a Baptist Church, and automatically looked for the nearest Baptist fellowship when I arrived. There wasn't one in the village, so I went along to worship in the local Methodist church. I'd never experienced the 'circuit' idea before, where one minister would travel round several churches, but I had many happy times there and learned a lot. My favourite speaker who came to the church was a Welsh gentleman, who always used unusual illustrations to convey his message. I remember returning to College after my first Sunday service. I bumped into one of my lecturers, who was coming back from the local Anglican church. He asked if I'd enjoyed morning worship. I said I had. He told me that they had had a sermon on the omnipotence, omniscience and omnipresence of God. His expression spoke volumes as I told him that ours was about a pig at a circus!

One of my friends was a tried and true Anglican, and was determined to help me find 'the way'. Her church was having a special outreach weekend and I was invited to go with her to the Sunday morning service. As we drove along, she told me that one of the things she was most looking forward to was the dance group. A dance group in a church service? I somehow couldn't quite imagine 'Saturday Night Fever' on a Sunday morning. I decided to sit at the back of the church, in case the experience was too much for me. The service went very well and then the six dancers appeared before us.

I have to be honest and say that I sat there with several handkerchiefs at the ready, prepared to stuff them into my mouth at a moment's notice. How wrong I was! I was deeply moved that morning, as I saw these girls worship God and express His Character in a whole new way. I realised how often I am suspicious of what is unfamiliar to me. As the church pianist played some of the more recent worship choruses, the dancers gracefully used their arms and feet to express the devotion in their hearts and on their faces.

I guess the greatest lesson I learned in my varied experiences within different denominations is that our God is working and moving wherever He finds people who love Him and want to know Him more.

One of the aspects of life at London Bible College or LBC, as we called it, that I found most enjoyable was that of the practical evangelistic teams. I led a team which took part in street ministry on a Saturday morning. We would drive into nearby Uxbridge and set up in a busy square in the town centre. We sang, painted, did short sketches – all sorts of weird and wonderful things. It seemed a healthy combination to have our heads in books and our feet on the streets. I'm not sure how culturally relevant our set-up was, but God blessed and used our enthusiastic efforts. It always amazed me how many people would stop and talk, often sharing really deep, sad things about their lives.

I began to feel so frustrated, seeing such need and not being able to meet it all. There were one or two good churches around but I felt these people needed more. It seemed cruel to me to encourage people to share their problems with us and then just deposit them on a church doorstep for two services every Sunday. They needed friends, constant support, and love.

In my final year at LBC I joined a new team. Every Sunday we went to spend time at the local boys' Borstal. At first, the boys were very suspicious of us but after some time they would open up and talk. So many of them came from almost impossible family backgrounds. I went through a really angry stage in my life. It seemed so unfair that so many people were born into terrible circumstances, with so much stacked against them. It reminded me of the Paul Simon song: 'Some folks' lives roll easy, some folks never roll at all . . .' The boys would ask me very difficult probing questions about God and love and life. I didn't always have an answer.

As I look back at my time at LBC I'm very grateful. I'm glad because of the people I met – the ones I liked, and those I didn't. The man I'm most thankful for is Gilbert Kirby. He had a rare combination of wisdom and wonder. He was a very well-read clever man, and yet he had retained a childlike wonder at the mystery of the gospel. He was very gracious and always had time for people. Even when we were coming out with what he must have known to be unmitigated drivel, he still listened. His sense of humour was a strength to all who came in contact with him. I'm so glad that we've remained good friends.

As graduation day loomed large, the question in all our minds was, 'Where now, Lord?' Most people were either bound for 'the ministry' or the mission field. I had come to feel during my time at LBC that God wanted me to use music to express His heart. How and where I didn't know.

The end crept closer still, and I had visions of returning to Ayr and working in Safeway! Friends of mine lived down in Eastbourne in Sussex. They had a very successful recording studio and I popped down for a few days to see them. Andy, the engineer, told me about a group who had recorded there and were looking for a lead singer. Their name was Oasis and they worked with International Youth For Christ. I said that I'd love to know more and he called them for me. The director, Ted Groat, flew over to London to audition me. I was petrified. I took all the music I had down to Hildenborough Hall, where he was staying. He was a very tall, skinny man. He sat down at the piano, took my music, and began to play. I gripped the side of the piano till my knuckles were white and started to sing. When he said I'd got the job, I nearly passed out at his feet. I was sure that I'd need to wait a while before I would hear from him – they must have been desperate! I just had time to go home for two weeks, buy travel sickness pills, and set off.

As I sat on a bumpy boat late at night, heading for Holland to join the rest of the group, watching a video of M.A.S.H. for the third time, an uneasiness crept over me. What was the Dutch for 'I'd like to go home now, please'? We arrived at Vlissingen in the middle of the night. A Dutch gentleman had driven down to meet the boat and we set off on a two-hour drive to my new destination. We didn't say a lot. I didn't know if he spoke English, and I didn't think my two

Dutch words – 'clogs' and 'Edam' – would get me very far. He dropped me off at a dormitory sort of place, which was filled with lots of Dutch girls who worked with YFC. It was a bit of a barn and it only had cold water. How I longed for my own room and my electric blanket!

They say things look better in the morning. They lie! Just kidding . . . with the break of dawn the old pioneering spirit re-emerged. I met Oasis at breakfast. There were six of them, from different countries, and they had already been together for a year. I felt a bit lonely at first, as the two other girls were both Dutch and were good friends.

The vision behind Oasis was that we should travel all over Europe, singing in schools, clubs and prisons, ministering as an effective evangelistic team. I asked who the leader was, and Ted said that we had yet to find a leader, but we wouldn't begin touring until we had. We did! They had a lot of bookings for us and no-one emerged to lead, so we left on our own.

Our first stop was a little village in France, where we would rehearse for two weeks. The average age in the village was about ninety-six! Every afternoon the whole population slept for about four hours and one great snore rose from Sleepy Hollow!

The style of Oasis was folk rock. I worked hard at learning all their songs. We travelled across Holland, Denmark, France, Switzerland, Belgium and England.

Our time in Denmark was really great. We were the first gospel group to be allowed to play in schools and clubs. The situation in that particular country was heartbreaking. Many of the guys in the band were approached by twelve-to fourteen-year-old prostitutes. Teenage suicide and drug addiction were so common. I can clearly remember sitting in the stage wings of a Danish club, waiting to go on, and watching people smash beer bottles against our equipment. I remember thinking, 'Lord, if you're planning to return any time in the immediate future, this may be an opportune moment!'

It was incredible to see God change people's lives as, night after night, we threw ourselves on His mercy. To know without a doubt that God's word is true, that His strength is made perfect in our weakness, the written word becomes life-blood. It seems to me now that the fruit of the Spirit is always produced in a contrary environment – peace in turmoil, joy in sadness, love in a hate-filled world. Most of our concerts were received very well, but there was one concert that will live in my memory for ever.

France was fairly new to gospel music and we were excited about our trip. I fell in love with Paris; it was winter-time but still beautiful. Our French promoter told us that our concert was taking place in a village in the mountains. He was excited about it, as it would be a new experience for them. How true!

We reached the base of the mountain at ten in the morning and began the ascent in our bus. We climbed and we climbed . . . and we climbed and climbed. By five o'clock it was dark, snowing, and we were still climbing. Eventually we could see lights in the distance and we pulled into the little – or should I say 'minute' – village. We asked several people if they knew where the concert was, but no-one seemed to speak any English. One old gentleman approached us and pointed to a building in the distance. We thanked him profusely and set off to put up our equipment. Looking back now, I can see the funny side, but to discover, after a seven-hour drive, that you are playing in the disused waiting-room of a railway station is stretching human endurance!

We looked for the power points to plug in our gear, but the only holes in the wall were where the snow was coming in! Refusing to be deflated, we decided that it was no problem, we would do an acoustic concert. So by eight o'clock we were all ready. We waited; eight-thirty, and still no-one had arrived. This is France, we thought; they arrive late. When the audience did arrive, we hoped that they would both sit in the front row, but they seemed to favour the rear! By nine o'clock we had eleven people in the room and felt that we could justify starting, as the audience now outnumbered the band. As it was cold, I could understand the big heavy coats, but the earmuffs were too much for me. We finished by ten and they all shuffled home, the average age being about seventy. No-one in the band moved; we stood there stunned for several moments. Eventually, deciding that it was either laugh or die, we dissolved. I've never been back to that part of France; things may have really improved. I guess I'll never know!

In many ways I found my time with Oasis one of the hardest periods in my life, having no pastoral leader and no real home. As the months passed and our travels continued, I became very disillusioned. We were always working, so we never got to church, never really took in on a spiritual level, apart from our own hurried quiet times. We usually began our days with a morning concert in a school, another at lunchtime, evening gigs, and eventually fell into bed after midnight. I really felt like a hypocrite. It's so hard to stand up and tell young people how they should live their lives when you're not doing it yourself! I began asking myself some difficult questions. What were my real priorities? Had my job become more important than my relationship with the Lord?

I felt in many ways that I had jumped into Oasis without actually asking the Lord how He felt about it. I remember a man speaking at College and saying that 'the need doesn't constitute the call'. I decided that I was going to leave. I told my European YFC Director and he was furious with me, but I'd made up my mind.

As I sailed back to England alone, I felt so empty. I'd lost all sense of vision and purpose. I just wanted to go home.

3

BACK INTO THE OLD ROUTINE

I'm so grateful to my mother for the way she allowed me to come home without demanding great explanations. I felt welcomed without pressure. It was good to be in familiar surroundings, when I felt such a failure.

After a few weeks of relaxing and catching up with friends and family, I woke up to the fact that it was time to get a job. I decided to abandon music completely and get a 'real' job! I scanned newspaper 'Situations Vacant' columns for weeks. Jobs were scarce, especially if you weren't trained as a poodle-clipper or didn't want to join the army! One day, despairing of ever finding anything, something caught my eye. The advertisement described a position working in a Christian children's home with emotionally disturbed youths. I immediately felt drawn to this opportunity. I had tremendous visions of sitting in an armchair, with poor misunderstood little boys at my feet. I would sing to them and somehow, by the consistency of my love, help them to find the Lord. I had definitely seen too many Walt Disney films!

I filled in an application form, was interviewed, and got the job. It was a residential post and I was to look after nine boys. The post entailed waking them up in the morning, getting them fed and off to school. They returned at about four o'clock and were mine until bedtime.

I was officially introduced to the boys on the day I moved in. I was impressed. They seemed so polite and friendly. Their ages ranged from twelve to fifteen.

The first few weeks flew past. We really had a lot of fun together. In the evenings I got permission to take them out to the cinema or a football match. We played endless games of snooker, a new sport to me, and discussed everything from music to manslaughter! The only mildly intimidating thing was that most of them were several inches taller than me.

One boy in particular really stole my heart. I'll call him Simon for anonymity. Most of the boys stayed at the school from Monday to Friday, and spent weekends at home. I used to dread Simon going. He would reappear on a Monday morning, very badly bruised and intensely quiet. I felt that everything we tried to build and develop during the week was ruined at the weekends. I knew that his dad simply got drunk and beat him up in mindless temper. Simon was fiercely loyal to his family, and invented all sorts of stories about falling downstairs and bumping into walls. Many of the boys caused trouble from time to time, but Simon ran away from the school so many nights I lost count. He was usually picked up by the police in the middle of the night, attempting to break into local houses. One day he jumped straight through a plate glass window and fell two floors on to a flower bed. Simon was not a popular boy at school and was perpetually tormented by the others. I'll never forget finding him hanging upside down, tied tightly by his feet to a tree, and covered in bruises and blood. I cried more tears over that little boy than over all the traumas of my own youth.

My greatest problem with Simon was finding a way to get him to talk to me. At night, after all the boys were tucked up, I used to go round and sit on their beds, and talk to them about their day. With Simon I would always hold his hand and pray for him. He seemed to like it and wouldn't go to sleep until I had.

One day I found the key to his heart. He was helping me fix a new lampshade in my room, when he caught sight of my faithful old Snoopy dog. He was fourteen years old, but he hugged that stuffed toy and gazed lovingly at a new-found friend. I allowed him to take it back to the dormitory and 'take care' of it for me. That night, as I sat on his bed, he began to tell the dog about himself in my hearing. He asked the dog to ask me questions – hard, heart-searching questions. I had to direct all my replies to this lump of fur! Many nights we would sit for an hour, holding a three-way conversation. I remember thinking, 'If anyone sees me here, I could be locked away for a very long time!' I learned so much about his true feelings and fears and hurts in those times. Once or twice I took him home with me on my free weekends and we had such fun together. We saw movies, walked along the beach, and laughed a lot.

As Christmas approached, we, the staff, began planning the nativity play. Two of my boys and one from another dorm were the wise men – definitely not type-casting. A very shy little girl was picked to be Mary. The only concern with the choice was that she seemed to find it necessary to visit the toilet about every fifteen minutes. We felt that, if we kept her time on stage fairly short, all would be well. Fools rush in where angels fear to tread, they say! Simon was playing the part of Joseph. The scene was to open with Joseph at his carpenter's bench, hammering some nails into a large piece of wood. Simon had insisted that he would use what he was already working on in his woodwork class. We simply hoped that the audience wouldn't notice that Joseph was constructing a skate-board! The action was to continue as he knocked three times, and Mary would appear and enquire about his health. We rehearsed and rehearsed, and then the big night arrived.

Many of our local dignitaries were invited, one or two of the heads of our organisation, and the proud parents. The curtain opened, and there was Joseph with his piece of wood. He knocked three times . . . nothing. He knocked again, a little harder this time . . . still no Mary. Every time that I see a nativity play now, the scene before my eyes is of Simon throwing his skate-board into the orchestra pit and enquiring, in many and colourful four-letter words, as to the general whereabouts of Mary. Unfortunately she was responding to another call!

When my boss suggested that we should take the boys on a little holiday, I was really excited at the prospect. We decided to take them to Loch Ness on a monster hunt! We set off, with our sleeping-bags and Wellington boots, and headed north. Loch Ness really was a magnificent sight. The boys had a great time extracting stories from the locals and believing them all – me too!

One day, out walking, we came upon a lovely little church and all wandered in. It was a Catholic church and at one end hung a huge picture of Christ on the cross. Simon asked me who it was and I told him that it was Jesus. 'Oh, no, it's not,' he retorted, 'I've seen the film.' I'm sure that Robert Powell would be flattered to know that his role in *Jesus of Nazareth* was so convincing. Then Simon told me he was off to the toilet. After a moment or two I thought, 'This is a really small church; they won't have a toilet.' Fortunately I was just in time to stop him relieving himself in the confessional box.

I decided, on returning, that the dorm was far too impersonal and dull; it certainly didn't feel like home! I saved my salary for a couple of weeks, then went into town with the boys and bought all sorts of new fittings for the place. We put posters up all over the walls, new bright lamps and light fittings, and some nicer cups and plates for breakfast. It really looked a different place when we'd finished.

I had been told that I would go through a 'honeymoon' period with the boys, when everything would be wonderful, and then they would really push me to see how far they

could go. I guess you can never fully prepare yourself for
problems that lie ahead.

It was a Friday night and I told the boys that they could
watch *Starsky and Hutch* on our little television if they
cleared up the supper things. They flatly refused. I made it
very clear that if they didn't there would be no TV, but they
thought otherwise. I cleared up all the supper things, and
proceeded to remove the TV set from the dorm. Three of the
boys grabbed me, as one pulled the television away. They
threw me on the floor and informed me that they would be
watching their favourite programme. I got up and switched
it off, and then it seemed that all hell broke loose. Hearing
the terrible noise and smashing glass, a male member of
staff came in and disentangled me from the mess, and sent
the boys to bed. I lay on my bed and wept. I felt such a
failure. All my dreams of being the fragrance of Christ to
these kids seemed to crumble before me and, instead of
love, I felt anger and fear.

The next morning I went into the dorm to find that all the
posters had been ripped to pieces, the lamps and shades
crushed, and all the china broken; we were back to a shabby
little dormitory.

That day I read a lot of the confidential reports on my
boys, and could only ache for their hidden hurts. How can a
boy respond to love when the word is meaningless to him,
when he's never felt secure, accepted or valued as an
individual in his life? How God must ache for the crushed
in spirit. The boys saw me crying as I looked around
at the shambles in the room, and silently they picked it
up and cleared away the mess. It was never mentioned
again.

Things seemed to move from crisis to crisis. One of our
saddest moments was when the quiet shy little girl who
was Mary in our play was removed from our residential
school after being dragged into the boys' toilet and brutally
raped.

One day there was a very timid knock at my door. I opened it to find a distraught Simon. 'I've killed him,' he said. My heart raced; what had he done? 'I thought he needed a wash and I put him in the machine.' He held aloft the remains of my Snoopy dog, which now resembled a ferret that had been run over by a tank!

A few years later, when I returned to Scotland, I did a concert in my own town. Afterwards, I was sitting in my dressing-room and someone knocked at the door. I opened it and was faced with a fairly tall, nicely dressed young man. I can't tell you how wonderful it was to see Simon again – especially when he told me that he had given his life to God that night!

All through my time at the school, I kept open my links with British Youth For Christ and when, a year later, they asked me to come and join them I felt the time was right. I had learned many valuable lessons with the kids, realising that of myself I had very little to give. I felt too that my understanding of human suffering was very limited, and at times there are no pat answers that will do.

I was very excited at the prospect of being involved in music again, especially as I knew that with BYFC I would be part of a team and in a learning situation. So once again I packed all my belongings into a couple of suitcases and headed south.

The headquarters of our organisation were in Wolverhampton, so I moved into a house there with three other girls. It was tremendous fun to be living with three relatively normal people! Sally was a school-teacher and one of the sweetest girls I've met. Lesley was working at YFC and preparing to get married. (If I ever see another copy of *Brides* magazine, I'll throw up!) Jan was into gymnastics and ate a whole packet of chocolate biscuits every day – a strange combination!

Youth For Christ's work in England is orientated towards

schools and youth clubs, and really exists as the servant of the local church. They had at that time about sixty workers in England. Most of the staff were localised and lived and worked with schools and churches in one particular area. There was also a national team of singers and speakers and evangelists available to be used anywhere in the country. I was part of this team.

In my first month or so, I did all sorts of jobs. The great hate in the office was when it was time to send out the dreaded mailing. It seemed as if everyone from Bangkok to Bognor Regis wanted a copy of our prayer letter and information sheet.

I had never been exposed to schools work before in any major way, but the opportunities were incredible. A few of us would go into an area for a week and work with a church evangelising the area. We were allowed to take lessons with all ages of pupils (from thirteen to eighteen). I found it very exciting, thinking up creative stimulating ways of expressing who God is.

It was shocking at first when I realised the incredible ignorance about real Christianity. I remember being in one school and taking a one-hour lesson with fifteen-year-olds. I asked first of all, 'What is a Christian?', simply to find out how much they knew. There was an embarrassed silence for a few moments, and then one boy enquired about the possibility of it being someone who only drank tea. Another boy suggested that it was someone who grew his own vegetables. The generation of young people growing up now in England has no church background, generally speaking. A couple of generations back, people at least had a Sunday School upbringing. In some ways our situation is frightening, but the challenge to find relevant ways of communicating the good news to kids who have never heard is awesome.

One of my first major missions was working with the evangelist Eric Delve and a singer called Barry Crompton.

We worked with a church in Leicester for a week. I caught the train from Wolverhampton and sat opposite a lovely old lady. We chatted for a while, until it was time for her to get off the train. I took her case to the door, opened the door, got out and put her case on the platform. She stepped off, we said goodbye, and I got on again. I'm so glad she never realised that, as she slammed the heavy door shut (and I thought she was a frail old lady!), my thumb was still in it. By the time we got to Leicester, my thumb was the size of a hamster! So I spent the first night at the emergency unit of the local hospital, having my broken bone set, and my nail broken to the let the blood out.

It amazes me how God can change our lives in such a short time. Barry and I went into schools during the day, singing and speaking, and in the evening Eric would speak to a packed house at the church. The first two days were such a struggle, with little to show. The next morning, as we met to pray, Eric challenged us on how much we believed God could do, how committed we were to seeing people's lives changed. We spent about two or three hours that day in the church, throwing ourselves on God's mercy and grace, praying for transformed lives. That evening we knew that the battle had been won. Eric challenged Christians and unbelievers alike to live as children of the King. As people flocked forward at the end of the service, Eric and I both left the pulpit and knelt with the people; God was so obviously in control.

On the last evening, Graham Kendrick came to do a concert. Extra lighting and PA were brought in, and I guess we were really stretching the power supply of the church to the limit. As he sound-checked his last song, suddenly everything went black and the music was silenced. 'What happened?' someone cried. I still ask myself how I was supposed to know that one little box of heated rollers could do all that!

Graham is someone who I came to love and respect tremendously. He and his wife, Jill, and their Dulux dog, Paddington, became great friends of mine. Graham had written a song called 'Triumph In The Air', which I later recorded, and it became the title of a mammoth tour of Great Britain. Clive Calver was the head of YFC, and he and Graham and I, with a band of poor, faithful, unsuspecting musicians, set off round the country for three months together.

One of the nice things about staying in people's homes is the friends you make all over the country, but there are moments you never forget. One night I returned to my hosts at about midnight, after counselling a couple for ages. We had a cup of tea together, and then it was bedtime. The man of the house told me that I was sleeping in the garage. I said that was fine; I assumed it had been converted into some kind of room – but, alas, no! He took his car out, and the wife put up a bed between the deep freeze and the lawn-mower. It was November, and it was so cold. Every half an hour the deep freeze would chug into action; sleep became a thing of the past.

A few nights later, my hostess was a charming old lady with a plethora of cats. As I climbed into bed, I noticed that about nine of the little moggies had followed me. I tried unsuccessfully to put them out, just as the lady popped her head round the door and said sweetly that she hoped I didn't mind the little dears, as this was their room! When one of them landed on my face at three o'clock in the morning, I'm sure my aunt in Vancouver heard me yelling.

In every meeting, we became aware of such incredible need, and bruised and broken people.

While I was with YFC, a national event called Spring Harvest was launched. The vision was to bring churches together from all across Great Britain for a time of spiritual renewal and celebration. I remember the first one so well. About 3,000 people gathered in North Wales for a week's conference. The morning Bible studies were wonderful, the services and concerts stimulating, but the evening events were life-changing. To hear all those voices lifted in praise and worship to God in Britain was unforgettable! Every night God called people to Himself for the first time, filled people with His Spirit, called some to the mission field, restored marriages, and so much more.

Dave Pope, a well-loved British singer, Graham Kendrick and I led the evening worship. At first I felt really out of my depth. My previous experience of being in an up-front situation had left me feeling such a failure. God spoke to me that week, through the ministry of men like David Pawson and Luis Palau. I began to realise that God was not asking me to struggle on in a vain attempt at success, but rather He was right here with me. As I started to see who I am as a daughter of the Lord, I began to catch the vision of what God could do in our land. The possibilities were limitless!

4

BURN ON

I was so happy working with BYFC. All dreams, and even the desire, of being a solo singer had left me. My best friends from Scotland, Raymond and Nancy Goudie, had joined our work. Together with one or two others, we formed the Youth For Christ Band – a catchy title, you'll agree! Our main desire was to lead worship at Spring Harvest and other conventions, and to be steeped in schools work. Our repertoire was pretty limited, so our concerts had to be fairly short!

One evening I was babysitting for Graham and Jill Kendrick. Just before they went out, Graham told me that he'd written a song but didn't really feel it was for him. He had previously recorded several albums but never written for other people. I asked him to play the song to me. As he played and sang 'Burn On', my heart soared. What a wonderful song!

One day an invitation arrived at the office for Sheila Walsh and band to play at a major convention in England called Filey. Instant panic! We weren't a band, we didn't know enough songs. I asked Graham if I could sing 'Burn On', and if he could possibly come up with any more. He wrote 'Here With Me'. We learned about eight songs and hoped for the best.

When the evening of our concert arrived, I was in a state of shock. The concert hall was packed with 1,500 kids – and

I couldn't remember the lyrics of any of the songs. As I sat behind the stage, with a tube of honey and lemon tablets and my Bible, I read a verse I've never let go of: 'They who put their trust in the Lord will not be put to shame.' I realised that it would not exactly change the course of human history if I made a total idiot of myself. The important thing was the attitude of my heart, and my desire to glorify Him.

In many ways the evening is still a blur. All I know is that it went well! I had never given any thought to stage presentation or movement; I simply did what came naturally! We had some nice lights and the odd smoke bomb or two.

The next morning I faced my first barrage of opposition as a singer. Most of the kids were ecstatic about the concert, but one gentleman pulled me to one side for a thirty-minute lecture. He called me a Jezebel, offended by my wearing trousers. He accused me of being someone who was seeking to pull young people away from Jesus, a person who was setting herself up to take the glory away from God. All that from one little concert! I was devastated. I ran back to my chalet and cried my eyes out. I made up my mind that I would never sing again. Raymond and Nancy found me, and together we looked at our situation and asked our Father in heaven for His input. In many ways I am grateful to the people who constantly question my work, as it encourages me to continually bring it under God's spotlight. Having said that, if I could find that man again, I'd punch him on the nose!

At that same convention I met the man who, ten months later, became my husband.

I've always been a bit of a disaster in the area of relationships, being an incurable romantic. Walt Disney has much to answer for! When most little girls see Cinderella for the first time, a dream is born in their hearts. In this fantasy world, truth and goodness always win the day when the beautiful young heroine is swept off on a snowy charger into the distant sunset. It always finishes there. You never see beyond the horizon.

This is a wonderful trick of Hollywood. The human imagination is far more potent than anything they can produce on the silver screen, and each person is allowed their own private fantasy.

Romanticism is a subtle kind of escapism, where no-one gets hurt, apart from the purveyors of evil.

My first experience of true love was a fairly limited one. I was ten years old and had a distracting crush on a boy in my class. As Valentine's Day loomed large, I decided that this could be my moment to bare my heart and soul. I didn't have quite enough pocket money left to buy a card, so I decided to make my own – far more personal, I felt. On the morning of February 14th, I crept into the classroom fifteen minutes early and put the card in his desk. As the school bell rang and we all poured in, my heart was pounding. Would he be moved to tears? Would he embarrass me by immediately showering affection upon me? He opened his desk and shut it again. He hadn't even noticed the card. It was half past ten before his eyes fell upon the snowy white envelope borrowed from my mum's Christmas card box. He ripped it open and almost fell off his chair laughing. He nudged his friend, and they both had to stuff handkerchiefs into their mouths not to be heard by the teacher. I was totally shattered. The whole future seemed meaningless. My only redeeming thought was that I hadn't signed it. On the walk home from school, my hero's friend ran past me and shouted, 'Jim thinks your card is the dumbest thing he's ever seen!' Life was at an all-time low.

I recovered two weeks later as I fell in love with the captain of the school football team. This time my affection was not unrequited. He wrote on his football that he loved me, and gave me an engagement ring that he found on the beach. Our relationship was an undemanding one and consisted of talking to each other at the dinner break. I never saw him outside school hours, but it was the deep understanding between us that carried me through!

When I was fourteen, I found myself sitting beside a Greek god in the English class. He was tall and blond, with beautiful blue eyes and a smiling face. English was my best subject, but I don't think I uttered a sensible word all year. I ran downstairs one morning to collect the mail before my brother could get to it, and spied a large boxed card. As I picked it up and saw my name, I realised that February 14th was upon us again. My heart missed several beats as I prised it gently open.

'My love for you is as undying as the sun, as strong as the sea, and soft as the rain.' I sat down on the stairs and gazed mesmerised at this effusive expression of love. As I sat in the English class that day and gazed lovingly at my poet, I felt that life had never seemed so rich. I wondered if he would say anything or expect me to approach him. I left it till four o'clock, when the final bell rang, and was just about to thank him when I felt a little tap on my shoulder. I turned to face a rather well-fed, corpulent little boy. 'I hope you liked the card,' he whispered. As the crystal doors on the horizon slammed in my face, I thanked him profusely and hurried home! Romance was shelved for some considerable time.

In my last year at school, I had a summer job working in the accounts department of a car showroom. Most of the guys who worked there were definitely out for a good time as far as any females were concerned. I think they knew that I was archaically naïve and they left me pretty much to myself. The person that bowled me over was the young deputy manager. He was a really nice man and we had lunch together once or twice at work. Just as I was leaving one day, he popped into my office and asked me if I would like to go out for dinner the next evening. I gladly accepted.

All that evening I swung between two posts: I really liked him, he was stunning to look at, but he wasn't even vaguely interested in the Lord. After a lot of heart-searching, I phoned him up and told him that I couldn't see him. He was marvellous about it. I was sad, but a little relieved.

London Bible College seemed like heaven on earth. There were two guys to every one woman – and all Christians! I went through several relationships in my first year, none particularly serious. In my final year, all that changed. When you finally meet someone that you feel you could spend the rest of your life with, all other relationships in the past fade into insignificance. That year was one of the happiest of my life. We were assigned to the same evangelistic team and, as he preached, I went with him to sing. As we prepared to leave college, it became very clear to me that our visions for the future lay far apart. He had a very clear idea of what he wanted to do with his life, and I did too – but they never met. All my friends thought I was crazy; we were a seemingly well-suited couple, but there are indefinable signs when you know something is wrong.

I never dated another guy for four years. When I met Norman, it was a totally new picture. He was executive director of Word Records in England.

The evening after my concert at Filey, he asked me if I'd like to have lunch two days later. I said I'd be glad to. When I told one or two of my friends, they were against it. They painted a very strange picture of him as an unreliable playboy, but I liked him and decided to go anyway.

We drove into Scarborough, a nearby seaside town, and found a lovely Italian restaurant for lunch. He asked me if my friends had reacted to my having lunch with him. I remember thinking it was a strange question but I said that they had.

That day Norman really bared his soul to me. He told me so much about his life. He told me how his mum had died when he was a little boy and that he had found her dead. When his father remarried Norman found it difficult to accept his new mum, and left home when he was fifteen.

I wondered why he was telling me all this, and then I understood. Ten years previous to our lunch, Norman had divorced his wife. She had been a lovely Swiss girl whom he had met and married within weeks, but it had ended in unhappiness for both of them. They separated; she met someone else and married him, and they moved to America with their new little boy. Norman told me of the tremendous sense of failure and the guilt of broken promises that had haunted him for so long. He shared with me the way the Lord had been dealing with him, drawing him closer to Himself. David Pawson, a friend of Norman's, had helped him immensely. I remember thinking that day, 'I really like you; I'm so grateful that you've been real and honest with me.'

We finished our lunch and drove back to the camp. When the convention was over, I went up to Scotland for a few days to visit my mum. The doorbell rang one morning and a man presented me with a beautiful bunch of red roses. I hadn't a clue who they were from as there was no card. With my history, I didn't dare believe they were from anyone exciting!

I returned to Wolverhampton to begin work again with BYFC. One day Norman called me and said that he had to come up to Birmingham on business and would I like to meet him. We arranged a time and place, and then I really panicked. He was so sophisticated and well-dressed, with a very flashy sports car, whereas I worked on a YFC salary and didn't even have a bike! I went out and bought a new outfit with a whole month's pay, and felt like a real twit in it!

We had such a nice day. We drove to Stratford-on-Avon and had lunch. He knew that I loved Shakespeare and we visited his birthplace. We ended our day back in Birmingham with dinner at the Holiday Inn. As we walked back to the car, Norman told me that he had sent me the flowers. He told me that he felt he was in love with me, but didn't want me to say anything. He expressed his concern that, if we became involved at all, it would be very difficult for me. I guess neither of us knew how difficult.

We decided to see each other when we could. It was quite difficult, as he lived in London and I lived 150 miles away – but where there's a will there's a way! The next weekend he came up and we drove to Wales. We had a great day and popped in to see some friends in YFC that night.

The next morning I was called into head office to explain myself. I was asked if I knew what I was playing at, associating myself with a divorced person. I was so confused and upset. I went home, and wept and wept. Why had I waited all this time to find someone and now, when I felt I was in love, everything seemed so sordid and wretched. When Norman phoned that evening, I told him everything and he said that he wouldn't see me again. I felt as if I was drowning. I cared for him so much – but was it just because our backs were up against the wall? I just didn't know.

Eventually I was told that, if I continued to see Norman, I would have to leave. I knew that I needed to get away from everything and everyone, and think for myself. I was given some money and I went into a travel agency and said, 'I want to go somewhere in three days' time, and I want it to be far away.' As I sat alone on the plane heading for North Africa I'd never felt so isolated. For ten days I fasted and prayed, and asked the Lord to speak to my heart. I wanted so much to do the right thing.

On the last morning, as I went across the Sahara Desert on a camel to watch the sun rise, I knew that I had made up my mind. I wanted to marry Norman and felt at peace.

I had no doubt whatsoever that what he had done was terribly wrong – but was it the unforgivable sin? It seemed to me that, had I became involved with a murderer who had repented and come back to God, there would be no problem, but because he was divorced he was to be shunned for ever. Had his wife still been on her own, I think I would have felt differently, but she was very happily married, with two little boys.

I went into our office and told my immediate boss that I had made my decision, that I respected his position and input and, if he wanted me to leave, I understood completely. They decided to let me stay.

The next few months were a mixture of joy and heartache. I had lost some of my closest friends, and yet I found such happiness with Norman.

I remember clearly the day we became engaged. He went out on his own and bought me a lovely antique ring and a red rose. I was so happy, and went to tell my friends, hoping they would understand. They looked at me with such hurt and disappointment in their eyes, and walked away.

We were married in July 1981 in my church in Ayr. Our families were very supportive. The wedding was very small, but it meant so much to us. We decided that the first part of our service would be a time of repentance before God because of broken vows in the past. It was hard for Norman, but I really respected him for wanting to be clear and open with people.

I have to be honest, and say that I almost left all of this out of my book, because I'm not proud of the mistake Norman made. But neither am I ashamed of the decisions we took. We both feel so strongly that a society cannot exist on broken promises, that when we make commitments before God they must stand; but we also serve a gracious, loving, forgiving Father. We're very against divorce; it's never right. However, I do not believe that in a situation such as Norman found himself in, the Lord wants him to be miserable for ever. My two best friends, who were most against our marriage, are now two of our closest friends. They were honest with us, and our friendship survived. The people that I have a problem with are those who pretended to be pleased, and yet took great delight in talking about us behind our backs. As God's people, we have to live in the light with each other. I was told by one gentleman that, if I married Norman, God would never use me again. God is not like that. He looks at our hearts and our desires, and reaches through our mistakes to touch our lives again.

Marriage is great, but I wish someone would write a book to get you through the first year! There are many times when you feel, 'What have I done?' There are times when it seems as if the person you thought you married was a myth, and the one that you find yourself with is a stranger. I guess it's all part of the process of growing up. The shock comes when you realise just how bound up your life has become with another human being.

We had many awful rows in our first year. I would leave the house in blinding tears, resolving never to go back. There came a time in it all for me when I discovered that, even at times when I felt as if the glamour and romance had faded, I really loved this man.

But what do you do as a young couple when you're going through a really bad patch? I guess the worst thing to do is to stop communicating. I used to be very bad at that and would sink into long silences. I felt as if I couldn't make Norman understand, but I've learned to try. If you can still talk to each other, you are halfway to resolving your situation.

There are times, though, for some couples – and we were like this – when you are simply unable to deal with the situation alone. We find it's very good to talk to a couple that we both respect. At times it can be very difficult, even embarrassing, but it is worth it.

We had one tour in the US that was an absolute disaster. The concerts went well but, due to some misappropriation

of finances over there, we lost every penny that we had.
Not only did we come home after three months' hard work,
having made nothing; we also had to take all the money
from our English account to pay bills that we should not
have had to pay. The tour took its toll on us in different
ways, and we returned in a terrible mess, hardly speaking
to each other.

Our fellowship in Cobham, where we had moved to,
helped us wonderfully. They advised us to rest for a couple
of weeks and not discuss our situation. Then, when we
were both rested and calmer, they allowed us to share our
hearts. Neither of us wanted to see the other's side, but
somehow having people there with us who loved and cared
for us both helped immeasurably.

Obviously these times are few and far between and,
praise God, getting fewer! One of the things I've learned is
that just because I'm not wrong doesn't mean I'm right!

When I got married, I suddenly had someone who was
very gifted in administration and management, and
obviously expected to be allowed to exercise his gifts freely!
We had many confrontations at first, but again the wonderful art of communication came to the rescue. We recognised
that in many ways our situation is unique, but basic Scriptural principles apply. There is no doubt in my mind and
heart that Norman is the head of our home, but we are, in
reality, a team. We've learned to discuss things and listen to
each other. In God's kingdom we don't have to struggle to
assert ourselves, but learn to live with each other.

After we'd been married for about three years, I felt as if
romance had sidled out the door. Norman had always been
wonderfully thoughtful. It seemed however that we had
moved away from this and I felt neglected. Ever so subtly, I
mentioned this one evening, and Norman appeared to
ignore me, which I took to be a good sign! The next day he
went out and bought a beautiful long-stemmed red rose.
We had a lovely candle in our bedroom, with silk flowers at

the base, and Norman set the stage. I was ironing late at night, and when I'd almost finished, Norman said he was going up to bed. I said I'd be up shortly. He went upstairs and laid the red rose across my pillow and lit the candle. I was watching a movie on video and got very engrossed in the plot. Norman eventually fell asleep, and woke up to see flames reflecting off our bedroom walls. The little candle had burned down and set fire to the silk flowers. He quickly put them out and, in disgust, put off the light and went back to sleep.

Some time later, I crept upstairs and, not wanting to wake him, I undressed in the dark and slipped into bed. As I laid my head on the pillow, a searing pain shot through my skull as I was pierced in several places by the merciless rose thorns! The best laid plans of mice and men . . . !

Norman is a wonderful organiser. After we were married I left YFC and we began to work together, with Norman planning our tours and road managing, as well as playing piano!

All my favourite American singers had recorded for a label called Sparrow. The president of Sparrow Records, Billy Ray Hearn and his wife, Joan, were friends of Norman's. We met up for dinner one evening before Norman and I were married, and I loved them. They were a very special couple, and Joan was to become like a mother to me in America.

A few months beforehand, the Youth For Christ Band and I had recorded Graham Kendrick's two tunes, and Norman played them to Billy Ray. He seemed to like them but, as I said to Norman later, 'He's not exactly going to say it's the worst thing he's ever heard, when we're driving him back to his hotel!' I never gave it another thought.

As our one single had been well-received, we decided it would be good to cut an album. Graham Kendrick came up with some great songs, and the record company came up with our budget. We realised that, with the amount of money we had, we would have to do it in about nine days, and also never eat lunch! Our engineer, Paul Cobbold, produced it. I sang most of my vocals between midnight and four in the morning, propped up against a convenient wall. 'Future Eyes' was the finished product.

Norman took my album and several others over to America to see if anyone would be interested in them. I was so excited when it was decided that Sparrow would release mine. My first USA tour was planned.

5

IT'S ALL FOR YOU

As we flew off to New York I was ecstatic! It had been decided that I would tour with one of America's favourite gospel musicians, Phil Keaggy. He lived in Kansas City with his wife, Bernadette, and their little girl, Alicia. We flew out, met his band, and began rehearsing.

Our first concert was a festival with 29,000 people attending! I was being put on in Phil's set as an extra; no-one was expecting me or had a clue who I was. When Phil announced me, I felt about as popular as a rattlesnake in a lucky dip! My music was definitely different for America. For the first two songs they just stood and looked at me, and then apparently decided that they liked it. We had only learned five songs, as I was simply Phil's guest. When the audience continued clapping, the promoter asked me to sing again. I told him I couldn't, as we didn't know any more! I ended up having to sing the same song twice – how embarrassing!

We had a nice bus to travel in. I couldn't believe that it wasn't a Transit van; it was a real bus, with real beds and a television! We began our tour in the South, in the buckle of the Bible belt. I'll never forget the first night, as I walked on stage in a silver and blue jacket, with what was later described as 'an unnecessarily glittery headband'. I couldn't believe that so many people needed to go to the toilet during the first song – but they never came back!

Afterwards, Phil and Bernadette tried to put me back together again. One of the band told me that he thought America wasn't quite ready for me yet; I told him I was perfectly prepared to go home and wait! The reaction was never quite as strong again as in the South, but the questions were still raised. 'Can a girl wear trousers on stage?' 'Is the gospel compatible with rock music?'

We travelled from Los Angeles to New York. What a country, with such changing scenery, and so many different hamburger restaurants! One day, at a concert in New Mexico, a lady asked me if I was aware of the devil's preferences. I said that I wasn't sure what she meant. Apparently she was referring to a song of mine called 'Fear of Silence', where I used red and green lights, and she was amazed to realise that I didn't know that those were his two favourite colours! I considered dropping the song, but a few nights later a six-foot-six man gave his life to the Lord, as he said that song summed up his story. The song stayed in.

The state of Kansas is a huge flat agricultural state. Right in the middle is a very little town where we did a very little concert! We stayed at what was probably the only motel in town, and all I can say is that, when I kept rabbits, their hutch was a lot cleaner. We were told that it was the pheasant shooting season, and it certainly seemed that many a pheasant had put up his last struggle in our room. I threw my bag on the bed and it moved. 'Norman, there's a beast in the bed,' I whispered frantically. He examined it closely and informed me that it was a water bed. In Britain we don't really have those – other than in one or two dubious houses! We didn't know that you were supposed to switch it on to heat it up. The hotel and our room were so filthy that, when I went to bed, I had more clothes on than when I was up. I didn't want anything to touch me. The bed didn't have enough water in, and every time Norman turned over I went out with the tide! At about four in the morning, we realised that we were both about to die of hypothermia, lying on this icy cold water in November. At that moment I would have gladly revisited the old lady and her swarms of cats!

We climbed out, put on as many sweaters as we could find, and lay on top of the sheets, pretending we were on a desert island!

We moved on to New Mexico. Albuquerque is a beautiful desert place, surrounded by mountains. The concert was packed and went very well. I was standing around at the end, speaking to kids, when a young couple approached me. The guy asked me if I believed in the 'super nine all the time'. I must have looked bemused, as the girl said to him, 'I told you she didn't.' I felt indignant about being written off for something I didn't even understand. As I probed deeper, it emerged that they were referring to the gifts of the Spirit – which I most certainly do believe in! Religious jargon drives me nuts!

I found it very difficult to handle, being judged by how I looked, rather than what I said. So many people seemed to have a problem with the fact that I had short hair, or used special lighting effects on stage.

I began to see that a lot of the problems were cultural rather than spiritual. In England, where so few young people go to church, the desire and need is to reach kids on the street in a way they can understand. In America, many of the kids are brought up to separate themselves totally from the world. Somehow between us we've got to find a way of being in the world but not of it, of communicating with our generation that there is a God in heaven whose desire is to know us. I have to say that I've come to love America and its people with all my heart. Perhaps, as an outsider, it's easier to be objective and see such things as an unhealthy worshipping of success in the nation that creeps into the Church, but the people are warm and kind and enthusiastic.

The gospel music scene in America is vast and well-established. In England the growth is much more recent, and influenced greatly by a young man in black leather with long blond hair.

> They say to cut my hair, they're driving me insane;
> I grew it out long to make room for my brain.
> Sometimes people don't understand
> What's a good boy doing in a rock and roll band.
> I know what's right and I know what's wrong,
> And I don't confuse it.
> All I really want to know from all of you
> Is why should the Devil have all the good music?
>
> *(Larry Norman)*

This song by Larry Norman became the cry of a lot of young Christians in the early 1970s. They felt that for too long the only music available to them was the traditional form of church music. Many of the young people growing up at this stage and finding Christ couldn't hope to relate to 'How Great Thou Art' on their stereos. Many of them had been saved out of the drug culture and needed new ways of expressing the same truths as the hymn writers.

The musical *Lonesome Stone* had an incredible effect on the youth culture on the fringe of many churches. Hearing what they knew to be true in a way that they could easily identify with and take friends along to was a breakthrough for our country. Some of the earlier artists to tour Great Britain were Jamie Owens, Second Chapter of Acts, and Barry Maguire. They were accompanied by 'A Band Called David'. The sound was revolutionary.

The hymns that I grew up with as a child were beautiful. The lyrics were profound and deep, but the language was often archaic and difficult to assimilate. Suddenly to hear music that spoke about our everyday lives and struggles in a modern idiom brought fresh meaning to Biblical truth.

I bought Jamie's first album when I was about seventeen and played the grooves off it. I got hold of the music book of the album and learned every song.

In 1973, an event called 'SPREE 73' was staged at Earl's Court in London. Dr Billy Graham was one of the speakers, and the incredible Swedish choir, Choralerna, made an indelible mark on the young enthusiastic audience. My friend Andree and I decided that we really wanted to go. At sixteen, the only way that our families were for it was if a responsible adult came with us. We picked on our poor minister, Edwin Gunn. We talked him into accompanying us and begged him not to have his usual cropped haircut before the event. It was just getting to a nice length, when we dropped into his home one day to see his wife, Morag. We raced back out again and tore along the main street – he was at the hairdresser's! As we arrived, the crew cut had begun, and no amount of attempting to embarrass him by making faces through the window and insulting the barber had any effect at all. We were disgusted!

SPREE 73 was one of the times in my life that seemed like a milestone. I listened to many wonderful speakers and teachers, inspiring us young people to shine for the Lord in our world. Much of the teaching was based on practical evangelism; thousands of us realised for the first time how to go about telling our contemporaries about Jesus. We were accommodated in church halls all over London. As we travelled back each evening, the sound was amazing. In all the tube trains and buses, hundreds of young voices were raised, singing about the goodness of God. As we travelled back to Scotland, we determined never to be the same again.

In 1974 five of us left Ayr in a little minibus to take part in another relatively new event. This creative arts festival was called Greenbelt. Little did I imagine at that time, huddled in our leaky tent, that I would one day have the privilege of sharing the main stage with so many people whose music I had appreciated for years. Greenbelt was totally unique.

Thousands of young people camped in a large field for a four-day action-packed event. There were morning Bible studies, seminars, and, from five in the evening onwards, concerts were presented on centre stage by five or six artists. It was there that I heard for the first time the lyrics of 'Why Should The Devil Have All The Good Music?' Larry Norman is a powerful communicator. His rock and roll was high energy and exciting, and yet when he spoke, almost in a whisper, people silently listened. I don't remember much more about the weekend, other than the challenge to go home and live out our faith in our own communities. These were all things that we had heard before, but it seemed as if, for the first time, tools were being put in our hands to do the job effectively.

When 'Come Together' was released, it sold more than any other gospel album in this country by a long way – over 100,000 copies. In the next few years, many solo artists and bands emerged in England. Adrian Snell, John Pantry, Mark Williamson Band, Nutshell, and many others, expressing in different ways their Christian beliefs.

Today, as I look at the gospel music scene in the USA and in our country, I can see that we have come a long way. But has it all been progress? I have hundreds of letters at home from young people who want to be gospel artists, to have a record contract, and to travel. My initial question to such people is often to ask them why they want to. Are they simply keen musicians who want to be able to improve their craft and are grateful for any advice, or do they feel that in some way God has called them into a 'ministry'?

One of the dangers of the gospel scene is that it is easy to be a big fish in a little pond. Standards have been raised immensely, but at one time you could learn three chords on the guitar and find yourself playing in the Royal Albert Hall. I hate to hear the comment, 'That was good for a gospel concert' or 'Good for a Christian record'. In music and art, things are either good or bad.

There was a time when worship music definitely got the 'poor relation' treatment. It was seen as simplistic and therefore not requiring talented musicians. To my mind, there is no greater kind of music than that which draws God's people together to worship and exalt Him. That is why I feel it is important to ask yourself, 'Who do I see as my audience?' Some people are Christians but feel no great desire to use their gift specifically to teach or challenge people on Christian principles. They are primarily musicians working at their craft in a living relationship with God. Some singers have a role in challenging Christians to remember who they are, to stir us up. There are many singers like this, who very effectively capture truth and aim their message towards our hearts. For some people, a great desire is born in them to use their natural talent to reach the unchurched in our country. Groups such as Heartbeat are tremendously successful in presenting the gospel clearly through song and testimony.

My feeling is that many musicians don't have any clear call or vision for their lives, and this is reflected in their presentation. If you feel that your audience is the unchurched, why play the gospel circuit? Surely we should be in the clubs, pubs and schools, fulfilling our roles where they can be best received.

The trouble is that the carrots that the gospel industry dangle before our faces never lead us in those directions. The people who are most effective in their ministries are those who are at home with their call, who know who they are, and are faithful despite criticism. Those who lead us in worship, such as Graham Kendrick and Noel Richards, fill a vital role in our lives as Christians. Singers like Sandi Patti and Steve Green, John Pantry and Adrian Snell, who use their gifts to challenge, encourage and bless us, put another piece in our jigsaw.

During the filming of the television programme *The Rock Gospel Show*, the group that most impressed my friends at the BBC was Resurrection Band. They live in a very rough, dangerous, down-town part of Chicago, and are part of a church called Jesus People USA. Every day they open a soup kitchen, where hundreds of street people come to receive their only meal of the day. There is no doubt about the calling in the lives of these people. They work, sleep and breathe sharing the gospel with the poor and needy. All these people, and so many more, have found their home within the musical spectrum. Where do you fit in?

Many people have asked if rock music is the most subtle piece of equipment in the Devil's toolbox. Steve Taylor's song 'Guilty By Association' takes a poignant look at present-day criticism of 'Jesus rock'. In Great Britain and America, various books have been published, heavily critical of the 1980s music scene. One gentleman was heard to suggest that to say one could have Christian rock was as blasphemous as proffering Christian pornography! Do we simply laugh these over-reactions out of court, or do they have a point?

I have a definite problem with the idea that the beat is intrinsically wrong. I cannot accept that this has any foundation in truth. Surely it is not the rhythm or the music that is wrong, but whose hands it is in? Satan created nothing but havoc. He has distorted many of God's good and perfect gifts. He has attempted to copy, but twist, God's moulds but in essence nothing came from him but evil. Our present youth culture's imagination has been firmly captured by the singers and musicians of our day. When Bob Geldof staged 'Live Aid', who else but a musical hero could capture the attention of half the world? To simply tell our young people that it's all evil and nasty, so stay away, is like telling the wolf not to throw Brer Rabbit in the prickly gorse bush!

I worry about the mentality that seeks to dissociate itself from the world. Jesus never did that. He walked in the gutters of His day and told the people that the Kingdom of God had come amongst them. We cannot go into our schools and theatres singing Kum Ba Ya and expect a captive audience! If we seek in our music to be real and honest, if we soak it in prayer and work hard to be the best we possibly can be, then I believe we have earned the right to be heard. So often as Christians we expect opportunities to fall in our laps, without being prepared to work for them.

I have tremendous respect for bands like Glasgow-based group Talking Drums, who put in the ground-work to gain credibility with their audience. I am not suggesting that we look at the biggest sellers in the secular charts and attempt to be a Christian version. If we believe that our God is by nature creative, surely we as His people have a different source to draw from.

My own particular focus of attention is twofold. I have a burning desire to reach the unchurched in our nation. Many people in Britain have rejected God for all the wrong reasons. You may say there are no right reasons, but God grants each human being the right to choose. My concern is that many people think they know what a Christian is and are put off. When I ask them to describe the God they have rejected, I say I would reject him too, but that's not the God I know. Everyone in our land has the right to see Christianity being lived out before them in power and truth.

My other burden is towards the 'Christian in knots'! So many young people live under incredible condemnation, striving to be perfect, and falling flat once more. The bitter circle sends them reeling. I must spend about half my time on the road simply listening to people. I never cease to be amazed that, no matter how far away from home I travel, the human heart is the same.

Being very much part of the music scene, I have, in all honesty, to express my concerns. There are many aspects of the world of Christian music that I am involved in that are, at best, unhealthy. In Britain and the States, various magazines carry charts recording record sales and most-listened-to tunes. Those who promote these would simply see them as an information service, supplying retailers with details of best-selling stock. The danger lies in the eye of the beholder. In America, and now in Britain too, we have a Gospel Music Association to serve and support our artists, record companies and radio stations. Every year awards are given to those who have produced albums that can be voted 'Best of the Year'. Other awards included top vocalist, instrumentalist, and many others. My problem with all of these things is the atmosphere it can produce among the artists, who now feel they are in competition. Please don't tell me that this is not so, or I'll shoot you at dawn! It is human nature that, if we feel we are up for something against our peers, our hearts pound and we long to be recognised. There is a definite place for encouragement and support of each other, but I'm not sure that this is the way. I know that these organisations are seeking ways of changing or refining their ways, and for that I'm grateful.

I have no problem with the gospel category in the 'Grammy' awards. I feel that, if the secular music world wishes to recognise excellence among Christian musicians, that is something to receive with thanks. The danger of charts and air-play singles is that we can allow these things to colour our music. The minute that you board the Ferris wheel of the gospel scene, one step leads to another. Your record company – understandably, from a business point of view – will advise or require you to record certain kinds of song that the more conservative radio stations will play. If they refuse to play your music, the kids don't hear it and don't buy the records. Sometimes you feel like screaming, 'This has nothing to do with anything that I believe in!'

It's not as simple as that however. Within the market-place on the business side are many godly men who are genuinely seeking to help put the music and the message into the hearts of young people. There is a tendency too among artists at times to think that we are the spiritual ones, and the nasty business types have no spiritual perception. Praise God that in many cases that's simply not true.

One of the things that worries me most about the nature of our work is the whole artist/fan relationship. I guess it's inevitable that, because I appear on stage in front of people and have some semblance of talent, I find myself with people who want to write to me and be my friend. The responsibility, to my mind, is awesome. So many people write letters baring their souls and asking for help and, no matter how hard you fight against it, the pedestal is dragged out. Many of the letters are moving and warm, some are very frightening. I had a letter from a young man who says he is determined to be alone with me some time and then he wants to die! A foreign gentleman thinks of me as his celestial queen! (Yes, my brother choked over that one too!) Sometimes fans will follow you all over the country, spending ridiculous amounts of money, in the hope of saying hello. This is where I feel that it is vital that we belong to a strong supportive Church. For too long the gospel musician has been a lone ranger, accountable to no-one. It's time to come home! There are still times when we'll let it go to our heads, but if we are lovingly covered by a church fellowship with whom we are brutally honest, the dangers are less.

There has been a definite attack on Christian marriage in the last few years. Musicians travelling on their own, away from husbands and wives, are much more likely to fall into immorality if no-one is aware of what's going on in their hearts. Responsibility and favour in the eyes of people can be a very positive thing if used wisely; if abused, it can be one of the Devil's most destructive tools.

One of my all-time favourite speakers is Tony Campolo. I once heard him address a large group, representative of the whole gospel industry. I've never forgotten his talk. He began by saying that he felt he was an unfortunate choice of speaker to address a group of gospel musicians, as he felt that at least half of all gospel lyrics were blasphemous! He helped us think through some things most of us had taken little time to consider. Many kids today who become Christians have no church background. They often respond to the gospel through contact with music and the concert circuit. Their first knowledge of God and the timid foundations that they lay are often based on the lyrics of the songs we record. If our material is wishy-washy sentimentalism, their picture of Jesus will be painted in those shades. If we lead them to understand a 'come to Jesus and everything will be wonderful' type of philosophy, will everything crumble when that proves to be a lie? The harsh reality of kingdom living is seldom painted. Taking up the cross daily and following Christ are difficult words to fit into pretty songs, and are left to gather dust on the shelves. Unless we allow people to come to grips with the very heart of the gospel, which was born through suffering, we have failed in our artistry.

At times 'art' is the last word that one would use to describe our music. Surely the role of the artist is to raise questions, to create a thought process, and allow people to follow through on their own. The type of parable that Jesus used to speak of the kingdom is in many cases a lost form. I believe though that, within our culture, a renaissance is taking place. Perhaps for too long our music has been purely propaganda or nostalgia. I am excited to see the prophetic edge returning to music in the church and nation. God has feelings about our world that they need to hear. It is the duty and joy of the artist to light a little flame in their hearts.

The young intrepid explorer

On holiday with a close
personal friend

At home with
the family

Giving my testimony during
my 'Peace, Man' days!

Just spotted someone trying to leave!

Norman and I at home for ten minutes

On tour with Cliff, Bill, Dave Cook and Tina Heath. We drew the long straws, the others went on horseback.

With Gerald, Anona and the boys. Tilly's the one with the big ears.

With Cliff and Alvin Stardust at the BBC Rock Gospel Christmas special

Cliff and I shooting the video of 'Drifting' – it certainly did.

With Steve Taylor at the start of our five months of touring together. We looked a lot worse at the end.

With Richard 'Jaws' Keel on a US chat show. I'm the garden gnome on the right!

Dinner with 'Lucy' from Dallas and her husband Dominique. He's Scottish too so we really had to fight over who'd pay the bill!

My 'If you take one more photo I could become violent' look.

6

CHILDREN OF THE KING

Life was getting more and more hectic by the moment. Our work was going well in America, the United Kingdom and the rest of Europe. Norman felt that we really needed a manager who would be based in England and could handle our affairs as we travelled. We only knew of one! Bill Latham managed Garth Hewitt and Nutshell, two of England's most popular gospel groups. He was also responsible for Cliff Richard's Christian charity work.

We approached him about being involved with us and discovered that Nutshell – or Network 3, as they were then called – were breaking up and so Bill was able to take on new responsibilities. I had actually met Bill some years previously. During my last year at school, I had a strange phone call from Dave Pope. He and his group, the Alethians, toured each year with Cliff, opening for him on his annual gospel tour for Tear Fund (The Evangelical Alliance Relief Fund). They had just discovered that one of their two girl singers was pregnant and would be having her baby in the middle of the tour that year! Dave asked me if I would be interested in replacing her.

I tried to sound calm, sitting down on the floor with the phone, biting my fingers so that I wouldn't scream out in excitement! It was all arranged. The Alethians were great fun to rehearse with. The other girl in the group was called Diane – or Dit to her friends. She was so funny:

her impersonations of Christian leaders and farmyard animals had me rolling around the carpet in agony.

I didn't meet Cliff until the first concert in Carlisle. I was standing at the back of the hall in the afternoon when he walked in. He came over to where Dit and I were standing and, in sheer panic, I ran to the nearest toilet and locked myself in for forty-five minutes! It seems so crazy now that he is such a good friend, but I just didn't trust myself to say anything to him in case it all came out back to front. By the third morning, I was so annoyed with myself. I thought, 'Here I am, ignoring this man and, for all I know, he could be wildly attracted to me!' (This was before the invention of mirrors!) I spent ages getting myself together, making my hair behave and applying just enough make-up for that 'casual' look. I came out of my room and looked over the balcony to the hotel reception. There he was, with the guys in the band. I prepared to descend the stairs *à la* Scarlett O'Hara. Unfortunately I tripped over my handbag, rattled to the bottom, and lay among a pile of suitcases. I felt about as sophisticated as the cleaning lady!

When I met Cliff again, through Bill, he fortunately seemed to have forgotten my *faux pas* of the past! He has become such a good friend to Norman and me. When it was time to record a new album, Cliff asked me if I'd like him to produce it. I was so excited! Working on 'Drifting' ('War of Love' in the USA) with Cliff, Keith Bessey and Craig Pruess was a wonderful experience. They were all so enthusiastic, making me believe that there is always more inside than you think! We recorded a duet, which was the title track of the album. A secular record company, DJM, signed me up, promising to release three singles, beginning with our duet. They really went to town on it. We filmed a video and had a press launch at the Grosvenor Hotel in London. I was interviewed by Capital Radio and asked whether I thought the song would be successful. Sheila 'Big Mouth' Walsh said she thought it would; in fact Cliff could record a duet with Miss Piggy and it would be a hit! After the song sank into oblivion, someone asked me what it was like to be less successful than a plastic pig. Words deserted me for once!

Later in 1981 I was asked by Bill and Cliff if I'd like to be the support act on Cliff's gospel concert tour. It was such a great opportunity to play to so many people, a large percentage of whom knew little about Christianity. I had been threatening for a year or two to diet, with no great deal of success. Norman and Bill felt that this was the moment. All I had lacked in the past was incentive! Rubbish! All their dreams of the butterfly emerging from the chrysalis were dissipated on the first day as the big cuddly caterpillar arrived for her sound check!

I began writing this chapter on a Monday. Probably for most men a Monday means a new week at work; for children it's back to school; but for women the beginning of yet another diet! I'm sure that I have read every book on the market even vaguely connected with the problem of health and weight control. I've bought books in England, Germany, Canada, America. In fact, as our friend Gerald Coates put it, if I carried all my diet books up and down the stairs once or twice, that would get rid of any weight problem permanently!

Where does it all begin? My mum is a good cook – not fancy, just really good home cooking. It's very much in the Scottish tradition to bake a lot. I have one aunt who is totally impossible; every time I go and visit her I come away feeling like the Michelin man! I developed a sweet tooth at a very early age. When I was four years old, my mum took me to see our doctor, as all I would eat were bananas and milk chocolate. Believe me, it hasn't improved a lot – but I've given up the bananas!

I seemed to escape gargantuan proportions as a child, presumably because I never sat down from first thing in the morning till last thing at night. When I went on to senior school, it caught up with me a bit. I was given the job of helping in the school tuck-shop. 'Ah, sweet mystery of life, at last I've found you!' It seemed only reasonable to me that I should test samples of any new products in the shop, and a few old ones to make sure that they were still as good. School lunches were a disaster. Every day for dessert it would be a six-inch square of stodge, the same stodge every day, with a different stodgy topping. I loved it!

I was only occasionally aware of being a bit too hearty for my height. At school sports day I was hopeless at running. I was never even second last, I was always last by a length.

One day after school my friend and I were in Woolworth's, buying sweets, when we spied a weighing machine. Beside it there was a chart showing what you should weigh for your height. We decided to have a go. I had never weighed myself and I must have been about sixteen then. We dutifully dropped our penny in and sighed at the obvious discrepancy between what should be and what was. We decided to think about it while finishing our sweets. I'd never even thought about dieting and so I really didn't have a clue. We went to the largest chemist in town and bought packets of slimming biscuits. I informed my mum that a new me was about to emerge, wearing a 'Do Not Feed' label. I woke up the next morning and ate two of these big dry tasteless so-called biscuits, and went upstairs to weigh myself on my mum's scales. Disappointment – I hadn't lost a pound! I faithfully stuck to this for two weeks and at the end felt very trim. My friend stuck it for a day and gave up, much to the delight of her fat mother.

All was well really until I went to London Bible College. For the first time in my life, I was living in a house with my own cooker. I took to it like a duck to water and ended up resembling Moby Dick! Not quite – but I did lose all the ground that I had previously gained. I had this wonderful little recipe for a Swiss apple pie, which was so wonderful that I made it most days. The trouble with being a bit overweight is that sometimes you end up spending a lot more than you should on clothes to camouflage your lack of protruding ribs!

When I was returning from Scotland to London after our summer break, my friend Andree came with me on the overnight bus. We were so bad for each other. We've probably eaten more together than in the rest of our lives combined! The bus journey lasted about ten hours. Looking back now, I can hardly believe what we consumed on that one trip. We both agreed to take a little packed food, in case we got hungry. I'm sure we could have fed the whole bus! We began our picnic as the bus pulled out of Glasgow, and brushed the final crumbs on to the floor as we arrived in Victoria Coach Station, London ten hours later. At one point in the night, I popped to the back of the bus where the toilet was located. Coming back, I noticed that all the bus was in darkness apart from two little lights above our seats, with the constant rustle of paper bags!

In Youth For Christ, things went from bad to worse. When you constantly stay in people's homes, it's so difficult to be on a strict diet. Most times we were only with people for one night and, if they have gone to a lot of trouble, it's very hard to abstain.

Then I got married! Norman decided that it would probably be a good idea if I lost a little weight, especially as I like to wear trousers on stage. Most of the time I agreed with him but, if things went wrong or I was under stress, I would rush to the biscuit barrel. The awful thing about trying to diet, but not really wanting to, is that it can make you very deceitful. I would cook Norman a nice dinner and sit down with an orange and a few grapes. He would be very impressed. Then I would go for a little jog. This jog unfortunately took me past the corner shop and I would walk back slowly, with a slimming magazine and a Mars bar.

All this time I felt as if a major battle was being fought

within me. I really did want to feel slim and well, but the struggle went on. I firmly believe that as Christians we need to be at peace with the Lord and ourselves before we can tackle this problem. I'm not talking to those of you who, over Christmas or the holiday period, gain a few pounds, only to lose them again at home, but rather to those of us who feel slaves to the kitchen or sweet shop.

In 1983 I decided that I'd had enough. Sue Barker, who had a villa in Spain, offered it to us for a winter break. I told Norman that I was going to take drastic measures, and he sat back, waiting to be convinced. For seventeen days I ate nothing. I drank a lot of fluids and lay in the sun and read. When we flew back into Heathrow Airport, I was like a stick. My friends were shocked, but said that I looked great. My problem was that I had really learned nothing. I was fine when I wasn't eating, but when I returned to food again I gained it all back. In about a month I put back on the seventeen pounds that I had lost. I was so disgusted with myself. I felt such a total failure. The self-condemnation piled on!

I then began something that I stayed with for over a year and began to show the signs of a bulminiac. Many people with this disease make themselves sick after their overly large meals. I took laxatives. I began by taking the normal dose, then doubled it. Eventually, instead of taking one at night, I was taking eight. Many times I would wake up in the middle of the night in agony. I was taking these little pills every day of my life because it made me feel thinner. Norman began to get really suspicious and, after discovering a few empty tubes, challenged me on it. To be honest, I was glad that someone knew, because I felt trapped. Norman realised, I guess, how great a problem this was to me and began to help me find a comfortable path to walk on. He helped me remember, not just in my head but in my heart that, just as I am, right now, God loves me and that he did too.

For people who have these problems, the roots are always deeper than a love of Smarties! We shared the problem with the pastoral group in our church and they were wonderfully understanding. They helped me to see that much of my problem was linked to the insecurity I often felt and the lack of love for myself. It was only when I began to come to terms with the fact that it really didn't matter if I was ever one pound thinner that it became a lot easier. I'm still no stick, but neither am I dominated by an area of my life so badly out of control.

There is a very definite danger of Satan preying on our weaknesses. We can find ourselves so preoccupied with our latest diet and potential binges that we become ineffective as God's people. When God told us to have no other gods but Him, He was not only referring to Krishna! God made all things and all things are good – until they begin to dictate how we live, and then we need to bring them under the Lordship of Christ.

I'm not proud of any of this. To be honest with you, I'd rather no-one knew about the stupid things that I've done. My motivation for sharing these things is that I ache for all of you who have struggled as I struggled. You could say to me that I was never really fat and that would be true, but irrelevant. When a problem exists for us, even though it may seem insignificant to others, that does not diminish its hold on our lives. I only know the feelings of hope and despair, struggle and disgust, common to all of us who try and change the way we look.

Please understand that you are loved, that you are unique and precious in God's eyes. The television screens and magazines portray pictures of glamorous skinny women, eating boxes of chocolate by the pound, and we feel cheated when it doesn't work. Far better to be a bit overweight but at peace and radiating the love of Christ, than to be model-thin and totally self-preoccupied and obsessed.

Perhaps I can share a few basic health tips that I have assimilated, which have helped me towards a healthier way of life. There are many wonderful books on the market which will help you choose a diet that is compatible with our lifestyle. Stormie Omartian's book *Greater Health, God's Way*, available through Word Records in England and Sparrow in America, is a wonderful well-balanced look at healthy living on a physical and spiritual plane. Audrey Eyton's *F-Plan* is also a marvellous book and very practical for busy mums. The book that I have almost adopted is called *Raw Energy* by Lesley and Susannah Kenton. This book, and many others, advise us all to increase the fibre content in our diet and lower our protein intake.

I am also a great believer in the short fast. A one-day-a-month fast would be good for all of us, as it gives our bodies a chance to rest. Perhaps, if you had time at home, you could even try fasting for three to five days. The effects are marvellous – clearer skin, bright eyes, and a bushy tail!

I would encourage parents to begin teaching their children at a very early age the value of good food. When I toured with Phil Keaggy, I was very impressed with the way his wife, Bernadette, took care of Alicia, their daughter. She kept a supply of healthy snacks handy – apples, little boxes of raisins, granola bars – and Alicia loved them. She occasionally had chocolate but didn't see it as a daily occurrence or associate it with love and comfort. I'm sure we can help our children to build healthy patterns for a lifetime. The school where a friend of mine works has withdrawn a certain kind of well-known sweet from its shop, as tests have shown positive links between this and hyperactivity in children. I'm not suggesting that we turn them into rabbits, but let's not give them problems that will live with them for years.

One of the greatest partners of a good diet is healthy exercise. The only exercise I used to take was dragging my weary body towards the kettle in the morning! This is a subject on which people have to find their own level. Some find running the best form to adopt. One of our closest friends, Ian Hamilton, who is head of Word Records in the UK, runs about seven miles every morning. Not for me, thank you! Women with a fairly regular lifestyle often are helped by attending classes and enjoy the company and encouragement of others. Once you get past the initial exposing of your leotard-clad body to other human beings, you've crossed the most difficult bridge. I can't do this, as I'm never home for more than a week at a time.

Some time ago I bought Jane Fonda's exercise tape, and it really works well for me. I bought a little machine to play it on, and use it most mornings in my hotel room. The first few mornings are difficult, but after that it certainly feels wonderful.

Tennis, swimming, walking, golf, cycling are all good forms of exercise. The important thing is to find something you enjoy. Why not start up a group in your own church for women and use this as a way of befriending your neighbours and sharing your faith?

Sometimes, when we are not happy with the way we look, we postpone any improvements until we are thinner. I really don't think that this is wise. Often externals such as laddered tights, down-at-heel shoes, clothes that haven't been pressed, are signs of self-disgust. I think when we begin to pay a bit of attention to personal hygiene and appearance, we feel so much better about ourselves and give off this feeling to those around us.

Sometimes girls take great care of how they look when they are single or engaged, and then let go once they are married. This seems a bit unfair. I know that we can say as Christians that we should love each other as we are and that inner beauty is most important, but we also have a responsibility to each other. I believe it adds to a marriage when both partners care enough to make a bit of an effort to please each other. Norman is really wonderful in this respect, and I love taking time out to show him that I care too. The important thing is to try to make the best of ourselves, not to attempt futilely to look like someone else. If you are a bit heavier than you would like to be, please don't fall into the popular trap of buying clothes that are a size too small. It's so much more flattering to buy a bigger size that hangs well, than to go for a more appealing size that is ill-fitting. Cut off the label if you must – only you will know! Try to avoid large patterns. Smaller patterns or self-colours are far more becoming on a fuller figure. It's amazing how much slimmer you look when wearing one colour top and bottom, rather than splitting yourself in half. If you are my height (five feet four inches) or smaller, high-ish heels are flattering if you avoid ankle straps. Try toning your tights in with your shoe colour for longer-looking legs. (That last tip was for ladies!) Make-up can either be very flattering, or scream at people as they walk past. To my mind, the more subtle the better. Pick eye colours that blend in with your own shade of eyes. Vivid blue can appear a bit startling on brown eyes. Clean, shiny, well-cut hair looks wonderful on anyone.

There are so many good books on all these subjects and, if you want to take it further, your local bookshop would be glad to help.

In all of this, remember that you are a child of the King, that your body is the temple of the Holy Spirit. Let's allow our bodies to reflect the peace and reign of the Lord Jesus Christ.

7

DON'T HIDE YOUR HEART

Norman and I had lived very happily in a little house in Croxley for the first year of our married life. We went along to Gold Hill Baptist Church, where the minister, Jim Graham, is a man we both love and respect. As our schedule became busier and busier, we were able to attend less frequently. I used to find it so hard when we were home. We'd go along to the morning service and the church would be halfway through a study that had obviously been marvellous, but we had missed out. We both felt that we needed more.

Norman came to me one day and asked me if I knew of a man called Gerald Coates. I had to say, in all honesty, that I knew very little about him, except that I felt he was perhaps quite a controversial character. I knew he was involved with what is known as 'the house church movement', which sounded highly suspicious to me! Norman told me that he wanted to put on an event at Wembley Arena and call it 'The Banquet', a feast of rock and praise music, and he wanted to involve Gerald. This seemed strange for Norman, as he didn't usually work with people that he didn't know well. He'd had lunch with Gerald once, but that was the extent of their friendship.

They began to plan, and it really was a fantastic weekend. Larry Norman, Andrae Crouch, Mark Williamson Band, Bryn Haworth, and many other musicians, including myself, took part. The speakers included Gerald, David Watson and David Pawson. We were led in worship, listened to stirring, challenging talks, and enjoyed the bands. I liked Gerald so much. There was something very real and unpretentious about him.

Norman and I had reached a bit of a brick wall financially. We wanted to travel and sing but we never made enough money to cover our costs. After praying about it for a while, we felt that, if we were serious about our work, we needed to invest any money we had in it. That meant our house! We decided that we would have the place valued and take it from there. That day an estate agent popped a note through our door, saying that if we wanted to sell the house he had a buyer! We phoned him and invited him round. As we talked to him about our work and our reasons for selling, he let us know that he was a Christian and asked if he could pray for us. It gets even better! We asked him to send his potential buyer round. She was an elderly lady. Norman showed her the house, as I was out shopping. He had a picture of me by the side of his bed and she said, 'That's Sheila Walsh, isn't it?' She too was a Christian and her son had my albums. The sale went through smoothly!

Gerald and his wife, Anona, offered us a base for a while when we were at home. They lived in Cobham in Surrey with their three boys. I have to be honest and say that I was very nervous about the arrangement. I didn't know how it would work to have two women in one kitchen. All I can say is that four years on we're still together! We lived in their home for three years and then, when things became easier for us financially, we bought a house together. Gerald discussed, with obvious care and insight, the particular problems that our lifestyle presented. He told us that it was clear to him that we would not always be able to fit in with the church's patterns, and so the church would accommodate us. That may sound fairly simple; it just doesn't happen too often!

Gerald and Anona, two of the 'elders' of the house church – Martin Scott and Mike Blount – and a lively Irish lady, Liz Coveney, formed a pastoral team to care for us. Each time we are home they meet with us, give us time to talk and share our hearts, and then they minister to us. Because of the depth of their commitment, Norman and I feel able to discuss everything with them. We talk over problems on the road, difficulties in our marriage, private failures and temptations. I cannot tell you how wonderful it is to feel that there are no dark corners in your heart or mind; that, even though you'll still be tempted, people are praying and caring. You may say, 'Fine, but my church isn't like that.' I would really encourage every Christian to have a few friends that you love and trust and can be honest with. Pray for each other, help and encourage one another. We need to be part of the life of the body of Christ. There is security in vulnerability and accountability.

One of the greatest lessons I have ever learned in life is to allow myself to need other people. For many years my life was a denial of the 'no man is an island' idea. I felt that I had taken enough on board to last a lifetime. With me, I'm sure there was spiritual pride involved too.

In my teenage years I saw many of my friends become involved in all sorts of unhelpful situations and I was determined to stay strong. Many times I would walk home from church, talking aloud to the Lord and telling Him He could rely on me, I would go anywhere and do anything.

As I grew up, I went through all sorts of agonies as a teenager trying to cope alone. My family have told me since that it was as if I had fallen into a hole that was so deep I was out of touch with them. I have vivid memories of sitting, staring straight ahead, as my mother tried to help and unravel my mind. She would ask me to talk to her, not to shut her out. I felt as if I was screaming inside, yelling for help, but it seemed impossible to verbalise my feelings. Problems always seem so suffocating when they are unshared, especially at night-time, as fear creeps in with the darkness.

One of Satan's most destructive lies is to make us feel unique in our despair. We feel that no-one has felt this way, thought these things, committed the actions that we have. Believe me, this is not true! I have worked with many great leaders and teachers who are respected worldwide, and the comfort I have received from their honesty over feelings of inadequacy and failure is immeasurable. We all have times of dry barren existence, when the memory of vibrant life is a distant one. The ability to confess our weakness and unbelief is often the first step home.

Unfortunately one of the greatest obstacles to this is sometimes the inability of others to accept us as we are. It is so hurtful if someone actually manages to open themselves up to another Christian, only to be met with disbelief that they could be so unspiritual.

For Christian and non-Christian alike, one of the most difficult issues in life is the problem of suffering. Why does it happen at all, if there is a God of love?

On my most recent gospel concert tour with Cliff, I spent time at the interval each evening meeting people and signing autographs. One gentleman hung back from the crowd, obviously wanting to talk to me on his own. He told me that he wanted to believe that there is a God in heaven, but felt desperately confused. Two months before the concert, his son, who was thirteen years old, went off to school in the morning. His father never saw him alive again, as he was knocked down by a train on the way home. This man asked, 'Is God loving, but not powerful enough to stop tragedy? Is He strong enough to do so, but not personal and loving enough to act on our behalf?'

One of my favourite books in the Bible is the book of Job. I have studied it over and over again, and received tremendous help. Job was a godly, righteous man, who actively sought ways to please God. The God he loved and trusted allowed Job's devotion to be put to the harshest of tests. He lost his possessions, his sons and his own health. His life was reduced to wretched misery. Job spends what we have as thirty-eight chapters asking God why. Most Christians assume the story of Job to be one of constant victory, because the verse best known to us is 'I know that my Redeemer lives'.

This is but a brief confession in a time of agony and questioning. I am so glad that we are allowed to ask questions of our God; He is able to handle our greatest doubts and fears. God, in a way, never answers Job's questions. He does something far more marvellous; He shows Job who He is. He asks Job where he was when He planted the stars in the sky and separated the sea and the dry land. Job is left with an overflowing trust in a great God.

Why are we as Christians embarrassed by grief? Why do we feel that in some way God needs our help to explain away tragedy in other people's lives? On a recent tour of America, two very dear friends of ours lost their son in a road accident. He was a wonderful, outgoing boy, full of promise, and yet his life was abruptly halted. As his mother and I talked on the phone together after his death, I could sense the frustration and heartache she was experiencing at the lack of sensitivity in other people. To say glibly to someone whose heart is broken that 'this was God's will, so pull yourself together' is the worst kind of religiosity. Sometimes the greatest gift is to say nothing, but simply to weep with those who weep. Instead, on many occasions, we feel obliged to offer a positive statement and, embarrassed by their despair, we turn away. When someone has been bereaved, they need to be allowed to grieve. This in itself is a healing process.

When my mother and father were younger, they attended a church once or twice that allowed no such privilege. At one meeting a young woman stood up and testified concerning the death of her son. She praised God for taking him home and rejoiced in his being in a better place. Everyone clapped and said, 'Amen!' Later that evening, as my mum passed this young woman's room, she heard her sobbing bitterly in the loneliness of those four walls. That is not spirituality. We need to be able to be real and open. Praise God that, as Christians, we can also say that death cannot steal our dreams away, that it truly is only the beginning. When we have been allowed to grieve and been helped through it, our faith is strengthened and we can say that 'all things work together for good to them that love God, to them who are called according to His purpose' (Romans 8:28).

One of the difficulties of being in 'full-time work' is that somehow we are expected to be on top one hundred per cent of the time. It's only right that people should be able to look to their leaders for strength and guidance, but where do the leaders look? When I first became known as a singer, I could see problems looming large. I would get letters from people extolling my virtues; one even said how the angels must be in awe of me! I secretly 'amen-ed' that one in my heart, but more along the lines of 'how did that one get in?'! Many singers and speakers land themselves in very dangerous positions because they have no-one to be wholly honest with. The problem with our kind of lifestyle is that so often we do not fit into the regular church structures. At weekends, when the majority of Christians meet together for fellowship and encouragement, we are 'on the job'. So many situations that develop into major problems could have been alleviated if help had been available in the early stages.

Our pastoral team encourage us to call them whenever we need help, so that a pressure can be dealt with before it becomes a crisis.

Last year I was travelling through New Mexico on a solo tour. My agent in Los Angeles had told me that a radio station had run a competition and the first prize was lunch with me. (I hate to think what the second prize was – a weekend perhaps?!) This meant that I had to get up at five o'clock in the morning and be at the tiny airport in the desert at seven to catch a flight to Albuquerque. I had asked if I had to dress up for this, and was told no, as it would be with kids.

That morning, the desert was fog-bound. Don't ask me how: I only know that the plane couldn't land. One was tempted to say, 'Tell him to come down anyway; he's hardly going to bump into anything out there!' but one didn't! By ten o'clock we were still waiting. Norman decided to call the radio station and tell them that we would be late. He came back white-faced and asked if I wanted the good news or the bad news. I opted for the bad news first to get it over with. He later told me it was just as well, as there wasn't any good news! My agent had got it all wrong. Instead of having a casual lunch with a few kids, I was speaking and singing to a group of 200 businessmen! I looked at my clothes; I looked at my chalky-white face in the mirror, and counted to thirty (ten would never have done it for me!). Just then the plane landed – curses!

As we arrived at this very plush hotel and were escorted to the top table, I felt like Daniel in the lions' den. Norman played for me and I sang a couple of songs, and talked about what I believe that God can do through music to reach our youth culture. They were a wonderful audience and I sat down, relieved, as another young girl got to her feet. What she had to show us that day has never left me.

A certain church in the South had recently been the victim of a desperate tragedy. Two of the boys in the youth fellowship had committed suicide. This girl was a reporter and had gone along to investigate the situation. The interview that she filmed with the rest of the young people in the church was heartbreaking. One of the boys told us his story. He had reached a point in his life where everything

seemed meaningless. The struggle to succeed and be someone was slowly strangling him. He knew in his head that
God loved him, but the reality of that seemed a million
miles away. Eventually, in desperation, he had gone to his
best friend and told him that he planned to end his life. The
friend tried to help and encourage him to hang in there and
succeeded in giving him hope. One of the boys who was
now dead was this lad's best friend.

I don't think parents and teachers understand at times
the terrific pressures that young people are under today.
That's why we need to help each other. There is no glory in
wandering around with a smile from ear to ear, saying,
'Praise God. Isn't life wonderful?' if inside we are falling to
pieces. It's only when we admit our needs that we can be
helped. We say we believe that we have been saved by
grace, and yet our attitude denies this. We cannot earn our
salvation by striving constantly for perfection. Our loving
Father in heaven has promised us grace for each day, and
the wonderful gift of forgiveness. As God's people, there is
no place for condemnation. When we allow God's love to
fill our hearts then we find we are serving Him because we
love Him, not out of guilt.

When I was a student at London Bible College, one of the
most widely talked about problems among the female
student body was the problem of being single. Many of the
girls were in their late thirties, and abandoning hope! Many
of them felt bitter and cynical and let down – understand-
able emotions. Our society is totally relationship-centred,
as is all life, but often the single person is excluded and
made to feel as if they have missed the boat and have no
useful role to fulfil. There is no easy glib answer and most of
us do want to be married, but I believe that there are
practical ways in which we can help each other. The
Scriptural teaching and traditional view is that the single
person has more time to devote to the Lord and to the

extension of His kingdom. My only worry on this front is that at times we, as the church and as married couples, can abdicate our responsibility towards the single person and leave them to the Lord! I know that there is no better place, but sometimes God asks us to fulfil our own prayers for other people. So many single girls have been packed off to the mission field and left to a lonely existence. We marvel at their dedication and know that one day they'll receive their reward, forgetting that they need us now.

I am a firm believer in the extended family. If you are a married couple, why not actively involve one or two singles in your home and lives? If you have children, they can really benefit from the input of other Christian adults as they are growing up. Norman and I love living with Gerald and Anona Coates – seven of us, and Tilly the dog! One of the things I love most about our lives is the relationship we have with Paul, Simon and Jo, their three boys. We've learned a lot from them, and I hope that one day we will be better parents because of our lives now.

For those of you who are single and unhappy about it, my heart goes out to you! During the four years when I never as much as went to the cinema with anyone, I experienced the tremendous aching loneliness that we can feel at times. Every time I went home I would bump into someone who'd ask me if I hadn't found a nice young man yet. I was ready to do bodily harm to the next enquirer! I prayed and prayed about it; I got angry; I got sad. I had times when I thought, 'Blow this, the world is full of nice guys, and here I am, waiting for a Christian version of one of them.' In my heart of hearts though, I wanted God's best. There are no magic tricks. It's not a case of saying, 'OK, I'm happy to be single' and up pops an eligible young man. At the heart of things we have to ask some difficult basic questions. Do we really believe that God loves us? Do you feel without a doubt that He wants the best for you and has your interests at heart? He does and He has!

Bitterness destroys the life of God in us, but trust and peace and honesty develop the kind of life that reflects His character. Happy single people make happy married people. So many people feel that, if only they were married, they would be content. With God's grace we can learn those lessons now and, if you do meet someone and get married, you will have so much more to give to your prospective partner. I'm not suggesting that you suppress your true feelings – quite the opposite. Have a friend or a family that you can share your hurts and fears with, and allow them to minister to you. We all need each other and together can show our society God's order and rule.

I spend a lot of time counselling young people who have become sexually involved with their boy friend or girl friend. The pressures towards this are so great now in our western culture. Our television shows make it seem very much the norm and, if you are sixteen and still a virgin, then something is wrong! The myth that you can live any way you like and not take the consequences is one that needs to be shattered for ever. God gave us sexual love as a deep expression of commitment within a secure relationship. We are drawn closer to each other and our mutual dependence grows. I have talked with many couples whose marriages are on the rocks. Very often they had slept with each other before they were married, and that bond took them into a deeper commitment than eventually either of them wanted. Sex is often tainted for people because of the negative associations they have. If we have, by God's grace, a lot of cold showers and long walks, waited until we are married, sex is a beautiful, exciting thing. God is not out to ruin your social life. He genuinely loves you like a father and wants the very best for you in all areas of your life.

My sister has two lovely energetic little boys, David and John. As I watch her tearing around after them, trying to make sure that some of the wallpaper remains on the walls and that the cat is allowed to keep her tail on her body, I often think that I'll settle for just having a dog! It must be increasingly difficult raising children in our ever-changing world. If you are a mum or dad, I'm sure your greatest desire is to see your children following the Lord. I have seen one or two Christian families where the children have turned away and fled in the opposite direction. The difficult balance is to find ways of sharing God's life and reality with them, but not sermonising at every available opportunity. When people are in love it's infectious. Our children can tell if our relationship with God is real and valid, or if we have grown cold in our own hearts. It must be equally difficult for kids who find the Lord and don't belong to Christian homes. Often parents are sceptical and unhelpful, at times feeling threatened by the change in their son or daughter. Our lives and actions should be our greatest witness. Words are relatively cheap and easy, but when we actively honour our parents and seek to show by the way we live that something has happened, the change is undeniable.

As Christian parents, it is good to encourage our kids at an early age to have an honest and real relationship with God. I'm glad that my mum didn't dampen my ofttimes wild enthusiasm, but tried to encourage me. The Lord always had time for children, and we must be careful to be aware of them and feed into their young lives. The Lord has often used Gerald and Anona's children to speak to us through their basic unquestioning faith and belief that God speaks today. The challenge for us, as the world offers our young people many exciting avenues to stroll along, is to find positive creative ways of fulfilling and stretching them. Sometimes all we are aware of is what they shouldn't be doing. Let's ask God for positive alternatives. The God we serve, His very nature is creative; let's find new ways of expressing life and truth.

In all our relationships we have so much more to offer if

we are not simply using people to fulfil a need in us. Only God can truly meet us where we are and allow us to build relationships that will last a lifetime.

8

FOOLED BY A FEELING

I get so many letters from people who obviously don't like themselves very much and wish they were like me. These letters always upset me, because I've gone through so many of the same feelings myself towards other people. One of the hardest things for me to accept in my life has always been me! For as long as I can remember I've had a complex about the way I look or don't look!

According to my mum, I was a naturally outgoing friendly happy little girl until my father's illness. It will probably seem hard to believe, but it took me almost sixteen years to come to terms with my feelings concerning the change in Dad and his subsequent death. I guess that, as a child, my understanding of his illness and how it affected his personality was very limited. The effect that it seemed to have on me was that somehow my dad's feelings had changed towards me and it had to be my fault. In my young mind I knew that he was a good loving kind man, so I must have done something to make him seem to hate me.

There was one particular occasion before my dad died, when he tried to hurt me, and I pulled his walking stick away from him and made him fall. As I have mentioned before, that experience turned into the nightmare that haunted me for years to come. I became much more with-drawn after Dad's death. I was very uncomfortable around other men in our family and would either cling to my

mother's side or sit in my room alone until they had
gone.

As I grew into teenage years I became a real loner and
spent hours sitting on my own or walking along the beach
at home. I sat many evenings, staring at the sea, almost
willing it to take me away.

There is a strange phenomenon (I'm sure psychologists
would explain it) that when you don't like yourself very
much you actively perpetuate that image. You seem almost
to send out signals saying, 'Keep away. Believe me, you
won't like me.'

When I was at high school, I found parties agony.
I wanted to go but I dreaded the possible outcome.
I can remember on one occasion saying to a girl friend
whose party it was that I hated dancing, and I would
put the records on. I was so afraid that, if I didn't do
this, I would sit on a chair all night, like a big cabbage,
and never be asked!

When I was sixteen, I had a terrible crush on the lab-
oratory technician at school. Any time I passed him in
the corridor and smiled at me, I turned a delicate shade
of crimson. Our school dance was approaching, and
one day two of the girls who were friendly with my
secret love told me that he liked me and was going to
ask me to the dance. I was so convinced that they were
laughing at me that I told them I wouldn't go with him
if he were the last male on earth, and that I'd never seen
so many spots on one human face. He never looked
at me again. If he has any kind of complex today, I know
it's my fault!

My other major problem was that I seemed to be a
collector of lame ducks. Somehow all the less attractive
boys in our class seemed to feel more at home with
me. Every now and again one of them would call me
up at home and ask me out, and I just couldn't say no.
I felt so sorry for them. I remember walking along the beach

one evening with a rather rotund boy who was three inches shorter than me, hoping that all my friends were at the cinema.

I had very long dark hair as a teenager. I decided one day that I needed a new image. My mum tried to talk me out of it, but I was determined. I decided that I would like to have curls cascading down my back. I made an appointment with a small local hair salon and tried to explain my vision. The lady seemed to understand and said that I needed it permed and cut in layers. I arranged with my mum that I would go by myself and then meet her and my brother Stephen in town afterwards for tea. I now know that she warned him that, no matter what I looked like, he wasn't to laugh. Some hope! The hairdresser seemed to cut and cut. All my lovely hair was lying on the floor. I said to her that I really didn't want it too short, but she assured me that it was the latest thing. How does one describe what it's like at eighteen to look in a mirror and see Hilda Ogden staring back! As I walked towards Marks & Spencer to meet my family, I could see that my brother was already on the pavement, holding on to a pole, laughing in agony. Such is life!

When I went to London Bible College, I got into a very bad habit that stuck with me for a while. (My husband would say I still have it!) I felt that if I wore something new then somehow it would make me more acceptable to people. Most of the students spent a large percentage of their grants on books. I borrowed their books and spent mine on clothes!

There were many times when I was growing up when, because I had a big sister, I wore her clothes after her. I didn't like this and was determined to make up for it. The ridiculous thing about this kind of treadmill that human beings can embark upon is that it never even works, and yet we keep on pedalling.

There were many times at college when I felt very

attract to the Christian guys there, but I was so afraid of becoming involved with anyone. In my mind and heart, whenever you gave yourself to someone and they became important to you, you also gave them the power to break you. The wonderful thing about God, that makes me love Him so much, is that He sees our deepest unconfessed hurts and His desire is to heal them.

One particular day at London Bible College changed my future. Each term we had a quiet day, with no regular lectures. We had a morning and evening chapel and the rest of the time was spent alone with the Lord. The speaker at morning chapel had chosen as his text Isaiah 43:18-21. The verse that jumped out at me was verse 18.

> Remember not the former things, nor think on the things of old; behold, I do a new thing. Now it springs forth. Do you not perceive it?

After chapel I went off to the woods near our college with my Bible and my daily Bible notes. As I turned to the assigned passage for that day, it was Isaiah 43, verse 18.

Later that day I was back in my room, lying on my bed, thinking about the verse, when a friend of mine popped in to see me. She was a very gifted artist and had copied out, in her exquisite copper-plate handwriting, the theme verse for our quiet day as a gift – Isaiah 43:18. I knew that God was trying to say something to me but I had no idea what. As far as I was concerned, my past was a closed book, with no bearing on my future.

I went down at ten o'clock to watch the news in the student common room, and suddenly became embarrassingly aware that I was about to burst into tears. I rushed upstairs and fell on my bed, and wept and wept. I felt as if I was groaning deep inside myself, but the cause of my grief was a mystery to me. Feeling I needed help, I knocked on the door of one of my friends at about midnight. I told her of my confusion and she suggested that we got down on our knees and asked God to speak. After some time she said to me that she didn't know too much about my family, but felt that God was trying to tell me something about my father. I knew that she was right.

As I began to allow God to gently open a long-closed door, I felt able for the first time to face the reality of a hurt that had coloured my life. I realised that, in all my years as a Christian, I had never prayed to God as Father. I guess that seemed a negative image. I went back to my room and all that night I sat on my bed, with my Cruden's Concordance and my Bible, looking up all the references to Father and rejoicing in them. I went to Mr Kirby the next day and asked leave to go home to Scotland for a few days.

My mum and I shed many tears together that weekend, as she answered questions concerning my dad that I'd never been able to pose before, but the tears felt good. As I looked through our photograph albums, at pictures of us all, I was grateful that I had had a father who loved me and had now found peace with the Lord.

I have shared this experience with people in concert a few times and on each occasion God has reached out to those with damaged hearts in the way that only He can.

What are the other things that make us feel so unaccept-able as people? I think for women it's often trying to be the Victoria Principal of Birmingham! Wherever we turn today we are confronted by image. A certain type of female is held up to us as the successful norm, and most of us feel we fall far short. Being five feet four inches tall. I used to go to bed at night saying to God that if I woke up to find myself five feet six inches I would be the best missionary that ever walked the roads of Scotland! (I was very young at the time!) Everything from TV soap operas to movies to magazines tells us that, if we look a certain way, our lives will be so much more fulfilling. Rubbish!

There are personality traits too which generally we can't

change very drastically. There is no point in trying to be the life and soul of the party if basically our nature is more restrained. If only we could learn to be relaxed and at home with who we are. The peace in our own lives and our genuine relationships with others would be so much stronger.

I know it's presumptuous of me to speak on behalf of the men in our community, but I really feel for you too. Perhaps it is even more difficult for guys who feel they are less than the norm. The macho image has been around in our society for a long time, and the modern-day heroes, from Superman to Rambo, do nothing to help the lesser-built man! One of my best friends at high school was a guy who was five feet three inches tall. I loved sitting beside him in class; he was so funny. He took ridiculous risks with his humour, which often landed him in terrible trouble, but he seemed to revel in it. I came across him one day, sitting in a field by our school, looking desperately miserable. We talked for a while and he told me that he was so fed up with trying to be funny all the time. I, along with my friends, had assumed that this was his nature, never realising the agonies he faced every day, watching couples pair off, and feeling excluded. He felt his worth was based on his being 'good for a laugh'.

Often our feelings lie beneath the surface,
hidden by the smiles we wear upon our faces;
emotions are concealed, we bear our sorrows on our own.
Grown-ups only cry when they're alone.

(Noel Richards)

The words of my friend Noel Richards' song ring bells in many people's hearts. Working with young people for a while in the home, and constantly meeting people all the time now, has taught me many lessons. Often the most seemingly aggressive people I meet are the ones crying out for help. People wear all sorts of masks to hide their hearts. I don't wholly believe that people are products of their environment, but some people certainly start with an unfair load against them.

My greatest heartache is when it seems as if people have gone so far that you cannot reach them. When I worked in the children's home in Scotland, I had a very attractive little boy in my dorm. He was very small, being one of the youngest. He really had a beautiful face, blue eyes and lovely blond hair. He seemed to keep himself to himself more than some of the other boys. I expressed to one of my colleagues one day a desire to probe a bit deeper with him, and was amazed when he told me to be careful as the boy was dangerous. I couldn't quite tie up in my own mind this sweet attractive little lad, with the image of supposedly the most volatile boy in school. Apparently one morning my predecessor in the dorm was having a quiet breakfast with the boys. He asked the one in question to eat up, but he refused. This poor innocent social worker put his hand on the table and said, 'Eat your breakfast.' At which point the child picked up a knife and pinned my friend's hand to the breakfast table. I made breakfasts a matter of prayer after that!

Some results of insecurity and poor self-image are inwards and, generally speaking, only hurt the person in question. With others this is not so.

For me, one of the saddest forms of outward action is jealousy. Jealousy hurts and confuses the people that it is aimed at but perhaps more disturbing still is what it does to the person in question. Jealousy is unreasonable. It seems to deny the facts and live in unreality. I have a friend who is extremely talented. Her talent is multi-faceted. There are so many natural gifts that she has that I will never be able to develop. The tragedy for me is that she is not able to enjoy them. In her mind the one or two things that other people are involved in and that are proving to be successful for them, rob her of any joy in her own life. These are areas that only God can change. We live in such a pressured, success-orientated society that it's not at all surprising that there are so many casualties amongst us.

The release came for me when I accepted the fact that I'll never be tall and blonde, that my cheekbones are not like Raquel Welch's, but that in God's eyes I am loved. If there is only one thought I can leave you with from this chapter, it would be that, as you are, right now, God loves you. He could not love you more. Don't try to be like someone else. Ask God what you can do with you! As Christians, we have to show the world that there is another way to live. Do we really believe what we say we believe? Do we accept that our priority as Christians is to be worshippers, to be taken up by the beauty and grace of the Lord Jesus Christ? For me, there is no more attractive person than the one who radiates the life of our Lord. I have one or two friends who, in worldly terms, would not be assessed as beautiful, but to me they are. They have found the real key to kingdom living. They are at peace with their destiny. This is something the world will never understand.

On a recent trip to a very affluent country, Cliff Richard and I spent some time with the 'beautiful people'. I came away grateful to God for the opportunity to share His life, but deeply saddened inside. Can there be a more disillusioning existence than the one they lead? To buy all the lies that society sells about the gold at the end of the rainbow, to climb and climb in its pursuit, only to find an empty pot. The myth is perpetuated, as few have the courage to say that it is empty and worthless. I am not against possessions; I have no problem with people being rich but, when it becomes a god, it is a faithless one.

It has amazed me recently how the pursuit of wealth and possessions seems to have crept into the body of Christ. I do believe that God delights to give His children good gifts and doesn't want us to live in need, but it would seem to me to have been carried to a ridiculous extreme. Church history has proved that the disciples of great men of God are often their worst publicity. They tend to take the teaching to extremes that weren't in the original master plan. I get disturbed when I talk to kids after concerts who are 'believing' for a flashy sports car or a swimming pool or private jet. These are not isolated cases. This doctrine, being a pleasant one, has spread fast! If, as some would have us believe, it is directly tied in with faith and true spirituality, why does it only work in affluent countries? In many poor nations, God's people rise at five o'clock in the morning to pray and praise for three hours before their daily work begins. I cannot, from studying the gospels, believe that we have a right to demand material extremes from God. Have them if you must, but please don't use the Lord as your divine excuse. I have many rich friends, who use their money wisely and are real stewards of their wealth. My concern would be with those who view God as a 'sugar daddy' in the sky. If our faith in God is always built on our receiving, we will miss out on the essence of our faith – sacrificial giving.

Our fellowship and a few others in England stage an event called 'Festival' each summer. It's a week of seminars and worship and teaching, and it's always very exciting. Norman and I had been in America for a month doing concerts and taking part in music festivals. We had flown from Los Angeles to Tampa, Florida, and then to London. We picked up our car and drove north for three hours to join in the last evening of Festival 85. We were physically drained and washed out, but we'd promised that we would be there.

I've never been in a meeting like it in my life. The evening went very well, the worship was inspiring, and the speaker, Dave Tomlinson, spoke in a way that was funny and challenging. After he sat down, another gentleman got up and spoke for a few moments about the three leaders on the platform. He commented on their integrity and vision for the Church in England. He said that he felt it would be appropriate if we took an offering to support them in their future plans. They placed plastic bins at the front and, as we sang, people came forward to give their offerings to God. It was a wonderful sight to see so many people flooding out, glad to give out of the fullness of their hearts, because God had blessed them in so many ways. After some time, Gerald stood and said that he wanted to say that God wasn't just interested in our money, but in our hearts and lives. He challenged us to examine ourselves and see if there was anyone or anything in God's rightful place of centre stage. I've never been so aware of an atmosphere of sacrificial giving as that which fell on us that evening. People were coming to the front and laying down 'Walkmans' because they felt that music was their god. Many laid down engagement rings, giving back their relationships to the Lord. One lady, whose husband had divorced her, put her gold wedding band in the offering plate. Several people put in cars, cameras – even a boat or two! People were offering their children to the Lord and asking Him to take them and use them. We are told that it is more blessed to give than to receive; that evening we knew it was true. When people are genuinely on fire for God, they will gladly respond to His prompting.

One wonders at times if the world has gone mad. The television screams at us that millions are starving, and in Beverly Hills women are having their French poodles dyed each day to match their own outfits. Cadillacs are being customised to accommodate open-air hot tubs, while, over in Calcutta, amidst death and human despair, Mother Teresa still takes her turn cleaning the toilets. Who has found the more beautiful life?

9

NOT GUILTY

About a year ago, I did a concert in the largest top-security prison for women outside of Russia. We had been invited in by a young Christian who worked there. The guys in my band were definitely not enthusiastic. Many of these women were murderers and were serving life sentences. We were told that they had no hostage ruling in the prison, so if any of us were taken by the women they would not bargain for our release. So encouraging!

The women began to pour in, about 400 of them. The guards positioned themselves around the crowd, some with guns. We began to sing and they really were very appreciative. We sang every song we knew, and they still clapped for more. We were reduced to singing 'He'll be coming round the mountain'! As I took a few minutes at the end to tell them about God, about the compassionate heart of the Father, they seemed to really listen. I told them that with God there is a tomorrow. Norman Barratt, my guitarist, sang a blues negro spiritual, and the women were with him all the way. We finished by telling them about forgiveness, about what Jesus actually did on the cross. I'll never forget the sight of those big strong hardened women with tears running down their faces. They knew that forgiveness is not cheap. They were all facing heavy sentences, and the idea of a man who steps into our place and pays the price meant so much to them.

I received a letter from a man who had become a Christian while on Death Row and was now serving a sentence in San Quentin prison. His letter totally devastated me. He spoke of forgiveness, knowing that he had years to spend in prison, but the forgiveness he had found was greater.

His letter was full of praise. He didn't ask if God would get him out of this mess. He simply rejoiced that he was a new man, with a future and a hope.

The feelings of guilt are learned at an early age. Almost as soon as a child understands the word 'no', he or she becomes attracted to the forbidden fruit.

For me it was garden peas! When I was ten years old, all my friends were taking their pocket money to the fruit and vegetable shop and buying pea-pods. They became the 'in' thing to eat. I used to get my spending money by ten o'clock on Saturday morning, and by five minutes past the hour it was gone. I believed in quantity rather than quality, and could buy eight blackjacks, two gobstoppers, four jelly snakes, and two white frogs for sixpence.

We used to gather on a Saturday afternoon and sit on a wall at a place called The Black Six. I became alarmingly aware that I was the only person not eating garden peas out of pods. No-one actually said anything, but I felt that my presence there was becoming an embarrassment to them. I decided to take drastic action. I went home, crept in through the kitchen door, and into the living-room. The coast was clear. I opened the top drawer of my mother's bureau and there it lay – her fat little purse. With my heart pounding, I opened it and extracted a sixpence. I raced off to the shop, bought the peas, and rejoined my friends. As I came home for tea that night, not only did I feel sick from eating too many little green vegetables, I felt sick inside. We had almost finished our meal when the bombshell dropped. My mum said that she really couldn't understand it. She knew that she had had a sixpence in her purse, and it was gone. I wondered why no-one else had become aware of the brass band that had just marched through the kitchen, then realised that it was simply my heart pounding in my head. I excused myself and went up to my room. What could I do? I felt that, if I told her, then she might not love me any more; but if I didn't, I would never be able to look her in the eye again. I went to bed that night, but sleep eluded me. At about eleven o'clock, I crept downstairs and let it all out in one huge sob. I told her that I had stolen her money, and could she ever forgive me. No cuddle ever felt as good as that one!

From this experience, you would imagine that I learned always to tell the truth. But unfortunately not! As a Christmas gift one year, an aunt of mine gave me a large glass Pluto dog, filled with bubble bath. I decided that I wouldn't ever use the liquid as it made the dog a nice colour. My mum was the missionary secretary in our church for a while, and on occasions she would entertain various people in this connection. One such evening arrived. Much of the day was taken up in baking and generally tidying up, so that everything looked lovely for her guests. We were delegated to play upstairs in our rooms. Just before the first guest arrived, I decided to take the glass dog for a walk. I began to gently bounce him down the stairs, when he slipped out of my hands and smashed into pieces. The bubble bath poured down the carpeted steps. My mum called out from the kitchen and asked me what had happened. 'Oh, nothing, Mum. I've just dropped my piggy bank,' I lied. I grabbed a towel from the bathroom and began to rub. As I rubbed, the liquid foamed and foamed until I was knee-deep in a white cloud of suds! I'm sure the guests saw the funny side. My mum certainly forgave me, but the lesson I learned is that lying only digs us in deeper.

I believe that one of the important things in our earlier years is to develop an openness and honesty in our relationships. Sometimes that's easier said than done. I had a friend who would go out and get drunk, and never tell her parents. They thought that she was a happy open daughter, but I knew the guilt that she dealt with. The longer that a situation like this is perpetuated, the more difficult it is to come clean. The shadowing partner of guilt is deceit. The trouble with living a double life is that we have to lie to cover ourselves at times. This process slowly erodes our self-respect; it is so destructive.

There also exists among us a strange unhealthy kind of guilt. I counsel so many young people on this area, which once was a problem to me. Many young people who are living in one-parent families, either through death or divorce, often develop a false sense of guilt. In my teenage years, I felt desperately responsible for my mum. I felt that, because she was on her own now, as it were, it was up to me to make her happy and never disappoint her or cause her any grief. There is a healthy kind of concern that we as Christians should have for our parents, and there is a concern that is guilt-based and becomes like a millstone.

I am so grateful to my mother for suggesting that, when I went to college, I chose one away from home. I think she felt something of my struggle and wanted me to know that she was not on her own, that the Lord was her strength. I talk to so many people who are the children of divorced couples and somehow feel responsible.

I read a really heartbreaking story just recently in a popular women's magazine. A famous football player had left his wife and four daughters to live with a younger woman. The youngest daughter was quoted as saying, 'Daddy, if you come back to us, I promise you I'll be a good girl.'

We will find this more and more in our society as the family unit begins to crumble. The children are left damaged, bitter and guilty. This kind of guilt, which is an unhealthy but natural reaction to the circumstances we find ourselves in, needs real love and care and prayer to help us over it. It was only really when I married Norman that he helped me to have a healthier balance in my relationship with my mum. We are great friends, which is something I'm very grateful for, but Norman helped me to take all my niggling worries over all the tiny details of her life and what she was thinking and feeling, and put them in God's hands. He loves us all more anyway.

The guilt needs to be confessed. I feel that we need to rediscover repentance, a genuine turning away from what we know to be wrong. So many people don't feel forgiven, and I think that much of that has to do with not knowing how to repent. The kind of society that we live in makes it seem as if any course of action is okay. The violence and immorality on our TV and movie screens makes sin appear glamorous. There are so many grey areas in our society, where life was once more black and white. We are told that basically we can live any way we like and get away with it. This is a lie. We genuinely reap what we sow, old-fashioned though that may seem.

Our minister used to tell us a story of a young boy who broke his mother's prize vase. He was so upset about it and begged her to forgive him, which she gladly did. A few days later he appeared with all the pieces of the vase, that he had taken out of the dustbin, and asked to be forgiven again. We cannot keep dragging our sins up before God's eyes when He has removed them from His sight – as far as the east is from the west. The thing that God asks of us is that we consciously turn away from what we know to be wrong. There is no way that we can do this alone. We need the help of the Holy Spirit to live in a way that's pleasing to God.

I sometimes feel though that we totally abdicate responsibility for our own lives. In Romans chapter 12, Paul describes us as called to be living sacrifices. The trouble with being a living sacrifice is that we can crawl back off the altar, or choose to stay there.

Once or twice, while I was working with the Social Work

Department just prior to moving South to study at LBC, I had occasion to visit psychiatric hospitals. As I walked through the wards, I saw the desperation and cry for help in so many people's eyes. Some seemed to have gone beyond that and were living in a pit, with no means of escape. I chatted for a long time one day to a Christian doctor, who told me that many of the patients were there because they could not deal with guilt in their lives. They had nowhere to take it. As Christians, surely this is one of the greatest pieces of news we have to offer to our world – the fact that the price has been paid!

I was at a conference recently with Gloria Gaither. She told the story of a parent who was suing the school system. The charge was that they had stolen her child's dreams. The teacher had been expressing to his class the futility of their lives, living under the threat of nuclear war. He told them that they had no future, no hope. When we are God's people, when we are forgiven, loved children, death cannot interrupt our dreams. It's only the beginning.

10

BREAKING THE ICE

I'd always dreamed of working on television. I felt that, if only we could have a programme that reflected the reality of the gospel, it would be dynamite!

I had just finished recording an album called 'Triumph In The Air'. My least favourite bit of every new record is the photographic session. I just don't have enough confidence in myself to 'give' myself to the camera. A producer from the BBC had called Bill, my manager, and sketched out a rough idea for a new show. They wanted to do a programme on gospel music and wondered if Cliff could help. Bill told him that I was a gospel singer and could perhaps fill him in a little more on the whole American and British gospel music scene.

So Jim Murray came along to the photo session for my album cover. I felt such a twit, posing for the camera, with a stranger watching me. We took a break and Jim and I talked for a while. I told him of a few ideas that I had and he just listened, not seeming too impressed. After he left, I thought, 'What a total mess I made of that.'

A few days later he telephoned and asked if I'd like to host the series. You could have knocked me over with a snowflake! We began to plan the first shows. It was great to be able to recommend some of my friends, such as Paul Field, Larry Norman, Bryn Haworth, Jessy Dixon, Adrian Snell, Randy Stonehill, and so many others. I found it refreshing and challenging to be the only Christian in the situation. It made me realise how often we use language that is very strange, at best, to the uninitiated.

I found it frustrating too at times. I felt that I wanted to say more about personal Christianity than was acceptable within the confines of a BBC music programme, but I felt it was a beginning.

Jim Murray and Caroline Stephenson from the show have become good friends of mine. Their input and patience with such a newcomer to television have been incredible. As the series progressed, it was interesting for me to read the piles of mail that were sent in from viewers. Many people who had no church connection whatsoever wrote about the fact that we seemed excited about God! Anglican bishops, Catholic priests, lay preachers, representatives from the whole gamut of religious groups sent in encouraging letters. I expected to receive a lot of criticism and didn't actually get as much as I thought I would. Some people expressed genuine concern that I didn't seem to be as positive as I perhaps could be. I tried to find time to answer all the letters and explain that, if I was to perpetually fly in the face of my instructions, we might lose the show altogether.

I'm sure that the time for change is before a new series begins. With the third series, I've expressed some changes I'd like to see made and hopefully we have ended up with a better-quality, more assertive television programme that will communicate to Christian and non-believer alike.

The one thing that has emerged from the whole experience that has upset me most is the way in which, as God's people, we deal with what we don't like in each other. A few letters accused me of only being in the business to bring glory to myself. Some said that I was obviously losing my faith and didn't love the Lord any more. These accusations hurt me more than I can say.

If Jesus had asked us to wear a badge declaring our faith,

we would gladly have pinned it on. If He had demanded that we all dress alike, it would have been a relatively simple thing. He chose the difficult thing; He asks us to love each other.

When the Lord prayed for the church, recorded in John chapter 17, His heart was heavy for those of us who would believe through the words we heard. He prayed that we would be one, just as the Father and He are one. Jesus said that in this way the world would believe that the Father had sent Him. Why should this have been such an incredible declaration of life and truth? Because without Him it is impossible.

It concerns me that, as God's people, we concentrate so heavily on the external. We organise massive evangelistic efforts. We stage concerts and sell our records and books. We buy T-shirts emblazoned with pronouncements of our salvation or the world's doom. We have Jesus socks, car stickers, and so much more. This is all fine and has its place, but Jesus said that if we loved each other the world would know and believe that the Father had sent His Son. I often feel that other religious groups put us to shame with their zeal and commitment, but we have at our disposal the promise of the Holy Spirit to live in a way that is pleasing to God. Everything else can be copied – and is.

In London on Saturday mornings you can't walk down Oxford Street without being accosted by one sect or another. In Los Angeles Airport, if you survive five minutes without a flower being thrust in your face and 'peace' bestowed upon you, it's been a remarkably quiet trip! Every other religion has its books, speakers, missionaries, records, but we have been given the blueprint for love.

I have been looking recently at the way that the Lord responded to criticism. Even when people were trying to trap Him, He still answered their questions, but seeing the motive of their hearts. His knowledge of the Scriptures and His truth and integrity angered those who were out to destroy Him. The lesson I've been learning is to be open to criticism and questioning, but to be firmly rooted in the Bible and in fellowship with others. The Lord spent so much of His time in committed prayer; He studied the Scripture texts available to Him. How much more do we need to re-learn these basic Christian principles of life.

There has been a reaction in our time against the traditional 'quiet time'. I honestly feel that much of this is healthy. I am against slotting God into fifteen minutes of our day and then feeling that we have fulfilled our responsibility as His people. I know that in my teenage years I used to feel under incredible condemnation if I missed a day. My feeling though is that, as with all reactions, the pendulum has swung too much the other way. I don't think it's wise to teach young people that, as we are saved by grace, we may as well just sit back and enjoy the ride. Paul encouraged his young friend, Timothy, to train himself in godliness, saying that physical training has some benefit, but spiritual training benefits in every way (1 Timothy 4:8).

Much of this has to do with our church life. If our meetings, teaching and celebration reflect the life of Christ, then a hunger will grow in people to know this God more. It is only as we draw closer to the Father's heart and learn something of our own worth that we can learn to love each other. Where there is no life and people are paying lip-service to God out of fear, boredom, or a hypocritical self-righteousness, negativism abounds. There have been many attempts at a national level to draw God's people together. One of the greatest of those, in my opinion, was Jimmy and Carol Owens' musical *Come Together*. They wrote a two-hour presentation based on Church unity. All the songs encouraged people to be real and open with their fellow believers, to confess weaknesses, and to grow in faith.

When I was sixteen and a member of our church youth group we got hold of *Come Together*. We were ecstatic; we really felt that this could be of service in our church. The generation gap was fairly minimal, as the older people seemed incredibly tolerant, but there was still room for improvement! We rehearsed and rehearsed; we even had a drum kit! Our first performance was to be in front of our congregation on a Sunday evening. We were very nervous but it went really well. We came to the part in the evening where, if you have anything against anyone, then you go and confess it to them and ask forgiveness. I couldn't think of anyone that I had anything particular against, which was just as well! As I saw the line of people waiting to talk to me, I realised that I would be holding up the evening's proceedings! I was shattered. I guess I must have been more of a pain in the neck than I thought I was!

'I just feel I have to tell you that I'm fed up with you always getting the best singing parts. I think you're a show-off and I don't like your hair since you've had it cut. I thought I'd tell you this, so that you can forgive me.' 'Why, thank you,' I said.

As we began to travel a bit with the musical, I used to dread that part coming up, and pretended to be praying on my own!

The thing I'm trying to say through all of this flagellation is that our criticism of others has to be in a way that they can hear and receive. It may well have been unfair that I sang a lot of parts, I may well have been the biggest show-off in the west, with a haircut resembling a Tupperware bowl – but it was all a bit much to handle on one evening!

I still have a reaction away from taking opportunities. If you are an 'up front' person at all, it often evokes resentment in other people. Sometimes it's a lack of communication and people are left thinking that we feel superior to them in some way – which is ridiculous. It drives my husband mad that, if I'm asked to do things, sometimes I'll run a mile in the opposite direction, screaming 'Unclean, unclean!' When I was in Youth For Christ, Clive Calver, the director, had a very strong policy on criticism. He felt that, before you shared your negative thoughts, you had to say three nice things about someone. Perhaps he also had been a victim of *Come Together*!

One of the great things about this musical was that it genuinely got people communicating, and God moved among us. Each evening, as we sang, we saw the Lord drawing people closer to Himself and mending wounded relationships and broken hearts. As a youth group, it united us in a way we had never known, and taught us a little of love.

My time at London Bible College was the first time that I had been exposed to very differing doctrinal beliefs. We had a little student coffee shop called The Odd Spot, which became the centre of controversial discussion. The groups were very clearly defined. We had the Calvinists and Arminians, the charismatics and non-charismatics, those who practised baptism by immersion and those who believed in infant baptism by sprinkling. I tended to feel it was healthy to discuss issues, but I was not prepared for the feelings that accompanied the issues. It was almost as if each group doubted the Christian commitment of the other. Why are we unable to differ with each other and still be united in love? I think much of it has to do with insecurity in our own faith. We hold on to our own beliefs and preferences and, if God is with us, then who is with you? I am sure that there are many things that are important to me and, when eventually I stand before the Lord, I will realise that they really didn't matter at all. The important thing is to maintain our own faith and worship in the environment that we feel at home in, and yet retain our love for each other.

I see very little of my friend, Andree, now. When we both married, our paths went in very different directions. She joined the Salvation Army and I'm with the 'house church movement', but our commitment to each other and our love has never diminished. We worship the same living God, even though some of the externals are different. The Lord is moving in our church, just as He is in her fellowship. I think it's so sad when relationships are lost when people are not able to allow each other to find their own spiritual homes, and end up feeling threatened by one another. Noel Richards' song 'Broken Hearts and Broken Promises' addresses the situation well:

Why didn't we apologise, admit that we were wrong;
we could have been more humble but we both came on
    too strong;
wounded one another and lost our faithfulness –
broken hearts and broken promises are all that we have
    left.

(*Noel Richards*)

The subtle thing about controversy within the church is the way that it eats into our time. We spend so long discussing our theological preferences, and on our doorsteps the world cries out for bread. If we could learn to leave what we feel we need to prove to God, and get on with the job of being light and salt in a decaying society, our time would be so much more wisely spent.

At the end of the day only God knows. There obviously is a place for speaking out against untruth. Some of the shocking statements by one or two of our bishops in recent times certainly need to be challenged. They are robbing the world of the very heart of the gospel. Whenever someone who supposedly speaks for God is heard to deny the virgin birth and the resurrection of our Lord, our voices need to be raised. When someone tries to rob us of a personal loving God and replace Him with an impersonal cosmic force, we have to take a stand. On these truths we have built our lives, and the heresy that would deny them has to be exposed.

I found it interesting that the first people to pick up on these points were not those in the church, but the press. The world is watching and can see through the sham of religion with no risen Christ at the centre.

The type of criticism that I feel we need to learn more grace over is when basically we are fighting the same battle, although at times with different weapons. When Norman and Gerald Coates decided to put on 'The Banquet', one young man decided that it was a waste of time and money, and wrote to all concerned, challenging them not to take part, and tearing the event to shreds. The motivation of those behind the event was called into question, as was what would be done with the vast financial profits. The truth of the matter was that it was a project steeped in prayer, and the financial loss was borne by the two promoters and their wives!

I am not saying that our projects should sail forth unchallenged. What I genuinely feel is that we can raise all the questions without passing sentence. We should be open with each other and happy to share our hearts, but sometimes we are never offered that privilege.

Some people feel strongly about rock music in a Christian environment. On my last American tour, we were met by pickets at the door. As people were arriving for the evening, they were handed a leaflet. I got hold of a copy and was horrified to read it. It accused Steve Taylor and me of dragging people away from God's kingdom and said that people who listened to our music would end up in hell. Now, you may not like our records, but surely that is a bit strong! It is senseless to the world.

On one of my *Rock Gospel Shows*, I had two artists who don't like each other. The studio staff were told to keep them apart. No matter what the justification for their disagreement, to those who are onlookers it is confusing, to say the least. One make-up artist questioned me on it, genuinely concerned because she had understood that part of being a Christian was to do with love.

Why is it that we find it easier to believe the worst about each other? Surely our natural bent should be to believe the best and give each other a chance to reply to open questions.

One of the most difficult jobs within the church has to be that of the minister. How many times people must sit at lunch on a Sunday, having 'roast preacher'! The whole teaching concerning the body of Christ shows us clearly that we are all gifted and have the joy and privilege of serving one another and fulfilling our spiritual roles. Too often in the western world the man in the pulpit is left to do it all. Sometimes he wants it that way – and I feel that is equally wrong. Ministers are men too! They will all be different. Some are gifted in evangelism, some in pastoral work, visiting the sick, or counselling one to one. The trouble comes when we expect one man to fulfil all these functions. Many a minister's heart has been broken and his spirit crushed through the lack of love and support in his own church. The title of Clive Calver's book put it this way: 'With a Church like this, who needs Satan?'

Those whom God has called into specific leadership roles have a responsibility towards their people, but the job is made so much easier with the love and commitment of a congregation. Many a minister's wife has found her position in life a lonely one. The popular teaching is that they should not pick out particular friends within a congregation, but rather remain on friendly terms with all. This seems to be denying them a privilege the Lord Himself enjoyed. He had the twelve disciples. Within that circle, Peter, James and John were His closest friends, and John is remembered as the one He loved most.

I had a very sad letter from a young girl in Ireland the other day. She told me that she had a terrible problem with smoking. She felt it was wrong for her and wanted to stop. Struggling on by herself seemed to be getting her nowhere, so she decided to ask the young people in her church for help. During a time of prayer and fellowship, she explained her problem and asked for their help. She was greeted by a shocked silence. As no-one seemed able to offer any words of encouragement, she got up and left, and has not returned. Her letter was a cry from the heart, saying, 'I know I'm wrong, but how do I get right?'

Somehow, as Christians, we have got to grow up and learn how to deal with each other as real people. We cannot expect to be a helpful witness to the world if we don't allow our own to share their situations in honesty.

We have a nasty habit of categorising sins into the not-so-important ones and the real 'nasties'. Often on our not-so-vital list are things such as jealousy, pride, anger, selfishness etc. Surely these are, in actual fact, far more destructive than the person who has a problem with cigarettes, If we really get a firm grasp on what Calvary is all about, that will change our hearts. None of us deserves the grace of God. Not one of us is good enough to earn a place in heaven. When we all stand before the Lord and look into His eyes, we'll all know that without Him there was no hope. Please, let's open our hearts and arms to one another, as the Bible says: 'Bear one another's burdens and so fulfil the law of Christ.' Our world is full of hurting people. Every time I do a concert, I am amazed at the number of kids who share their deepest hurts with me. When I ask them why they haven't shared all this with a Christian friend or leader, the answer is always the same. They know that, if they did, people would be shocked and disgusted, and they would be made to feel like such failures. It is only when we are able to be real and confess our sins to each other that we can be helped.

We need to let the world see that we are fighting the same battle, leading a thirsty world to the fountain of life.

11

LIGHT ACROSS THE WORLD

I believe God is on the move in Great Britain in a new and exciting way. It's been a real privilege to work with Luis Palau a little in this country and see the way that he can reach kids exactly where they are. Mission to London in 1984 was a tremendous project, as hundreds of young people gave their lives to God on the football pitch of Queens Park Rangers in London. I have never experienced anything quite like Dr Billy Graham's missions in 1984 and 1985 in Great Britain. To see massive sports fields and stadiums packed to overflowing with 30,000 or 40,000 people each evening was a humbling sight. As I sat on the platform on the first evening, watching 4,000 people making Christ their Lord, I knew we were at the beginning of a major revival in our land. A television company was filming the proceedings and, as a young cameraman left his post to join the throng at the front, a colleague warned him that he could lose his job. His reply was that he could lose his soul and that would be a far greater loss. An eighty-year-old woman was asked by her counsellor why she had come forward. Was it to re-dedicate her life, a first-time commitment, help in her family – what did she want? She said, 'Everything I can get.' We, as the Church, need to be ready to receive the people that the Lord will bring into the kingdom in the next few years. The tide has turned in our land, and God is giving us another chance!

My first experience of evangelism was the night they hooked me! Although I was one who benefited from this kind of public evangelism, I never for one moment intended to do the same for anyone else. I assumed that it was a job you were given – e.g. bank manager, fire-eater, evangelist! My faith was very real to me and I wanted my friends to know, but I didn't know how.

The Heralds came back to our town a few years after my conversion, and I decided to become involved. Before a mission of this magnitude, our minister made us understand the possibilities open to us. He encouraged us to specifically pray for one friend and believe God to work in their life. I had a friend called Fiona who was really great fun. She had a lovely voice and we'd taken part in competitions together. I prayed and prayed that she would find the Lord for herself. God was very gracious in allowing me to see the first one that I'd actually interceded for come into the kingdom so soon.

When I was about sixteen, our church youth fellowship was very lively. We used to go down to the sea and sing choruses, and speak to people as they passed by. We had one real character among us. George was determined to catch fish for Jesus, whether they were ready to bite or not! He made up an enormous wooden placard, proclaiming that Jesus is Lord, and marched up and down, singing at the top of his voice. His enthusiasm put us all to shame, even though his terminology was at times unconventional. He announced to the world at large that Jesus' blood washes whiter than Daz or Omo!

We had a club on a Saturday night and would invite people to come in off the streets. My friend and I invited all the nice-looking boys to come in, in the hope of converting them!

In the last ten years I have seen tremendous changes in our country. It seems as if the youth culture has moved off at a tangent, and methods that would have worked at one time are no longer culturally relevant. One of the things that has often concerned me is what we are bringing people into. Many times I'll go into an area with the band and do a concert and God will really bless the event. Sometimes I'll ask people to respond to God and see fifty to a hundred people come forward. The sad thing is if the churches in the area are not able to meet the needs of the new Christians. I, have now stopped giving a public invitation, unless I am actually working with a church and know that they will endeavour to disciple the converts. I wonder how many people have been sadly disillusioned after making a public confession and then being left to struggle on alone. I know you can say that God will still take care of them, but it is cruel to show someone that there is another way to live and not help them to find the way. I have talked to people who tell me that they've tried God and it didn't work. They are often the casualties of those types of situation.

For the last eight years, I have been involved in evangelism of one sort or another. My firm belief now is that evangelism is the role of the local church. There are one or two marvellous exceptions – men such as Dr Billy Graham, who is so obviously anointed by God for a special task – but on the whole it's up to you and me.

There is nothing so infectious as someone in love. Two of our closest friends are Steve and Debbie Taylor. He is a tremendously talented singer/songwriter and she is a gifted artist. When they got married, they seemed to carry an entourage of invisible violin players with them everywhere they went, looking at them, the air was so obviously filled with music! As they sat and gazed into each other's eyes, a large armoured tank division could have passed by unnoticed. All joking apart, it's a lovely sight when a couple are so obviously in love. On a local level, this is where evangelism begins. In some ways it is easier to stand on a street corner passing out tracts, hoping that someone will read and be saved; the difficult thing is to live it in front of all our friends and families.

In our church in Cobham we try to live in a way which shows the reality of Jesus to the village. We are encouraged to befriend people who are outside the Church. Often Christians have no non-Christian friends at all. I don't think that this is very healthy. I believe that, wherever God has put us – in our homes, educational establishments or jobs – we can live the kingdom way. Actions speak far louder than words.

It's very refreshing to see the way in which Anona, Gerald's wife, takes opportunities to share the Lord within the circles in which she moves. If you are a woman and feel tied to the home, and not so able to involve yourself in church activities very much, why not have a coffee group in your own home?

When Clive Calver moved south to work with the Evangelical Alliance, his wife, Ruth, soon began contacting her neighbours and inviting them in. In the natural course of events, she was able, in the relaxed atmosphere of a home, to tell how Jesus had changed her life.

A couple of girls in our church run herb and spice parties. They ask a few Christians to invite their neighbours and unsaved friends along. They demonstrate the use of the various products in cooking and have them for sale. At some point in the evening, one of them will speak for a few moments about the difference that God has made to her. I am always amazed by the genuine interest shown by most people. Often we are afraid to open up about our faith, but we have to remember that it is good news! I'm sure we would be shocked by the statistics given of people 'converted' by the Moonies, Hare Krishna Movement, and many others in the last few years. They don't imagine for a moment that people won't be interested and, day in, day out, parade the streets, selling leaflets and talking to people. We have the truth, the only way to God – let's not make it the best-kept secret in the western world!

Sometimes our attitude towards the unbeliever is unhelpful. To make a person feel like a second-class citizen because they have not yet found the truth is very wrong. We should be, as the saying goes, 'just one beggar trying to show another beggar where to find food'.

In the last year or two in Cobham, we have begun to learn one or two things that have revolutionised the face of our witness. At times our 'head knowledge' of Scripture and the practical application of our daily faith are miles apart. We are told so clearly in the Bible that we should be engaged in spiritual warfare. There is a battle going on in the heavenly places between good and evil. It is the Lord's desire that everyone enters the kingdom. It is Satan's intent to stop them. Sometimes we fail to see the hold that he has on the lives of those around us. He can blind their eyes at times to the reality of who God is. If people have been involved at all in witchcraft or any sort of dabbling with black magic, ouija boards or tarot cards, these things in themselves can be a major stumbling-block.

My upbringing was as a Scottish Baptist, and I am so grateful to God for the training ground that proved to be. In our fellowship in Cobham, we have been learning and seeing for ourselves what God has for us today. For a long time, the issue of the 'charismatic movement' was a red hot one. Do you speak in tongues? seemed to be the question of the day. Praise God, that no longer appears to be the case. We are discovering in our church just how vital the gifts of the Spirit are in combating the forces of darkness. We approach evangelism now in a totally different way.

In our house groups we will decide on a street or area that will be our particular concern, and then we will gather together and pray. I don't simply mean that we will ask God to bless our efforts, but rather ask Him what He has to say about the people who live in these homes. Often, through the gift of discernment and specific words of knowledge, we will be made aware of the influences and problems that hang over the homes for which we are interceding. I found this a very strange idea at first and imagined myself sitting down, trying to conjure up ideas of what people might be into! It may all sound a bit too mystical for you too, but why would it be difficult for God to reveal the hurts of a broken world to His people when they ask Him? If the Lord reveals specific needs or dark influences, then we will fast and pray against them. The battle should be over, to a large extent, before we hit the streets. People are often the innocent pawns in an evil game and we, as God's people, can pray for them to be released.

We have seen the difference in our house-to-house visitation. The receptivity and warmth of people has been amazing. Often we have shared things with people that God has told us about them. The gospel is not ours to keep. The world is crying out for something that it can depend on, something that's worth living and dying for. When Jesus was ministering on this earth, He performed many miracles and said that those of us who believe in His name will see greater things happen (John 14:12). For too long as God's people we have abdicated our responsibility in the realm of the supernatural, and hundreds of young people have rushed into the arms of the occult, where they can see something happening. I'm not suggesting that we all get into little high-powered groups and begin to manufacture faith that is not there. Work within where you find yourself right now.

David Pawson was a wonderful help to me on this. It's no use praying for someone's healing if we cannot possibly believe for that. Don't stand in our street and pray for the inhabitants of all the homes to come rushing out, crying, 'How shall we be saved?' if that's not within your faith! Begin in a small way. Pray for what lies within your existing faith and, as God honours that prayer, your faith will grow.

If we spent as long on our knees weeping over our towns and cities as we do planning new methods of evangelism, I believe the spiritual temperature in our country would soar. Sometimes, when we hear of the incredible revivals happening in other nations, such as Korea, we try to capture their formula. What we usually find is a group of faithful people who believe God and spend hours in prayer, praise and worship. God has told us that He will honour committed sacrificial prayer, but still we look for new formulae.

Gerald's middle son is called Simon and he's a real lad. He is the inventor of many and wonderful stories. Time-keeping is something with which he seems to have great difficulty. He is also the centre of many unusual happenings. He'll be coming home, genuinely on time, and be met by an escaped tiger, or attacked by a low-flying bird that carries off his watch and so he, as a good steward, has to find it! One evening, when we were all at home for once, ten o'clock had come and gone, but no Simon. We all began to speculate as to what could have happened. 'He might at this very moment be rescuing a baby from a river,' suggested one. 'Or giving the kiss of life to an asphyxiating cat,' proffered another. At 10.40 p.m. Simon walked in. 'Where have you been, Simon?' Gerald gently enquired. 'I was leading two of my friends to the Lord,' he replied. We all held our breath but, sure enough, fourteen-year-old Simon had been helping two of his equally wild school friends into the kingdom. The privilege belongs to us all. I am so glad that God constantly shows us that it's not always the wise and the eloquent that He chooses to use. No matter how hopeless you feel, how unable to say anything that will change another's life, remember it's not us who are special, but the God who lives in us.

Worship plays a powerful part in our sharing the life of God with others. We fairly regularly have 'Friends' Evenings', when we take the opportunity of bringing new contacts along. We always begin with a time of worship and praise. Many times, after people have become Christians, they'll remark on the powerful impact that the music and dancing and obvious enjoyment of God had on them.

Two of our dearest friends in the world are Barry McGuire and his wife, Mari. They are living now with their two children in New Zealand, but we stayed with them for a week when they lived in Denver, Colorado. We saw a lot of movies, did a lot of shopping and ate a lot of pizza! One night, long after the children had been tucked up in bed, we spent an hour or so, praying together for God's guidance on our lives. As we prayed, Barry shared a picture with us that he saw clearly before him. The scene was a large ocean. To one side lay a beautiful cruise liner that was very slowly sinking. There seemed to be three types of people on board. There were those who knew that the ship was going down and didn't care. Some knew and were panicking, but saw no way out. And there were those who didn't even realise. On the other side of the picture, a little lifeboat was bobbing on the surface of the water. The people on board were so relieved to have been rescued and were congratulating each other on a successful mission. It seemed to us that God was saying this: the world was the liner and the lifeboat the Church. We held the means of escape but had allowed a great distance to develop between us. We believed that the Lord was telling us to go back and tell them that there was a way out. Some would laugh and carry on with their drunken party, some would listen but decide against it, but others would gladly come. That picture has never left me.

The Bible encourages us to be in the world but not of it, and I believe that so often we, as the Church, have done the reverse. Perhaps this would be more true in the US, where the Christian population is much greater, but we in Great Britain cannot cry innocent. At times we meet together in our own buildings and sing to each other and give talks to encourage each other. We pray for the nasty world, but hope it doesn't crawl too close. The ideal was that we should spend our time, individually and corporately, before the Lord, equipping ourselves for battle, and then be the fragrance of Christ in the streets. We tend to keep the world at arm's length and yet all too often adopt its standards and values of selfishness, jealousy, pride and greed. I hang my head in shame at much of the exclusiveness that we are party to. We make Christianity seem like a club, rather than a lifestyle. I understand that Jesus pins, badges, socks, teabags (yes, gospel teabags, folks!) etc. are only the trappings that some people like to deck themselves in. My concern is that they become a poor substitute for the fruit of the Spirit in our lives and on our faces.

It's always very exciting when a well-known personality announces that they have given their lives to God. This has been happening more and more in the music scene on both sides of the Atlantic.

When Cliff Richard called a press conference and told them that he had been born again, he informed them that he would be withdrawing from the secular music scene. Many Christians wrote to Cliff and told him that they were glad he had come over to our side, and fully expected him to make a break with the pop world. After a lot of counsel and prayer, Cliff felt that this was wrong and told people he was staying in! I cannot think of a Christian in Great Britain who has had more of an effect on our nation than Cliff, simply because he has such a natural platform in his art form. He showed the world that it is possible to live in the world of rock and roll, and be in touch with the living God. Some Christians are still very critical of him, doubting his integrity. I'm glad he's been able to weather that. Some of his fellow artists have not. It's a sad reflection on our view of what a Christian is that, whenever a singer professes faith, we want to turn them into a John Stott or an Arthur Blessitt overnight! Why do we feel a need to stick these people, who are in reality babies in the Lord, in front of the world and expect them to be expert in apologetics? What they really need are a few people who will love them as they are and help them as they try to get to know God better.

12

NO ALIBI

In the summer of 1985 I was involved in a project on abortion with Melody Green, the widow of the American singer Keith Green, Second Chapter of Acts, and many others. Several musicians had been contacted by Melody and asked to sing on a recording called 'Fight The Fight'. The song was written by Annie Herring. Each of us involved was given an information pack, telling us in honest, if graphic terms the practical reality of abortion. As I looked at pictures of large plastic bins filled with tiny, but very identifiable babies, I was shocked to the pit of my stomach. I sat in my room that day and wept. I wept for us all. For the agonies of some of the pregnant confused women, for the silent screams of the little babies, but mostly for the aching heart of the God who created each tiny life. Only He knew what potential lay within those children lying in a senseless heap of humanity. The trouble is that we like to think that they are not human; they are cells; they are things – anything but children. Those of us who know the Creator have to face the fact that this is not true. 'Thy eyes beheld my unformed substance; in thy book were written, every one of them, the days that were formed for me' (Psalm 139:16).

> Who will speak up for the little ones,
> helpless and half-abandoned;
> they've got a right to choose life,

they don't want to lose.
I've got to speak up;
won't you?

(Phil Keaggy)

The lyrics of Phil Keaggy's song spoke poignantly to me when I heard them. Abortion is a very sensitive issue. Many people, Christians included, feel that surely in some cases it has to be justified. I used to feel that way. I used to think that if I, or a future daughter of mine, were raped, we should be able to stop the tragic life coming into the world. I can no longer feel this way.

Melody is hoping to gather a petition of over thirty million signatures to give to the President at the White House, demanding that legislation be changed. In Great Britain we have a time limit beyond which an abortion cannot normally be performed, but in the US the baby can be killed the week before it is due to be born.

What can we do to help the terrible suffering? In England, organisations like Care Trust, with Lyndon Bowring, are constantly working to change things. They would be glad of your help. On July 4th, 1984, American Independence Day, Andrae Crouch, Russ Taff and I took part in a concert sponsored by a church in Oklahoma. The money raised from the event went to beginning an exciting new project. The church decided to build a place for single girls who are pregnant and don't want the children. They will be cared for throughout their pregnancy and, when the baby is born, it will be adopted by Christian parents.

Some people say that it is unfair to expect young girls to endure the trauma of childbirth. Scientific and psychological research has positively shown that the horror and shock to the system of abortion is far greater.

Childbirth is at least a natural process, whereas disturbing the secure growth of a child in the mother's womb is totally contrary to nature.

On a recent concert tour, we travelled down the west coast of America. One evening I spoke about the problem of abortion in our society. I was really trying to encourage the girls in the audience to be responsible for their lives and for their actions. After the concert a very pretty blonde girl sat in her seat long after the auditorium had cleared. I packed up my stuff, told the guys in the band to go back to the hotel, and I sat down beside her. She sat with her head in her hands for half an hour, not saying a word. I prayed that somehow God would help her to open up to me. Eventually she told me her story. She had become pregnant and didn't know what to do. Fearing the reactions of her parents and friends, she went along to an abortion clinic alone. She wasn't a Christian and felt that this was the easy and only answer for her. Her question to me was, 'Why do I feel so guilty?' She told me that she didn't believe in God, in life after death, in judgment – so why was her life now a torment? She had sleeping pills from her doctor, as she could no longer fall asleep without a little help. She was angry, she felt bitter and cheated. 'Why don't they tell you you'll feel this way?' I don't know. Why don't they? She had decided one day in desperation that she would tell her parents. They were Christians; she felt they might help her. Before she had plucked up enough courage to spill her story, they announced that they were getting divorced, and that she could go and live wherever she wanted. She never told them. As she sat and wept bitterly beside me, I told her that someone knew about her abortion before she told me. I told her that someone had already paid the price for her crime. The very author of life had stood in her place to be punished for the death of her child. Some time later that morning, as we held hands and prayed together, she laid her pain and misery at Jesus' feet, and gave her life to Him.

Forgiveness needs to be accepted. We'll never understand it, never deserve it, but it's there for us.

In the Garden of Eden something's missing from the tree.
Adam says, 'Don't blame me'.
Eve says, 'That's not fair!'
Hey, listen! There's something hissing over there.
No alibi!

(*Graham Kendrick*)

'Am I my brother's keeper?' Cain's words ring through history and disturb our twentieth-century consciences. Many times in our evangelical history we have tried to shrug off the burdens of the world and its current problems, but they won't go away.

I used to find it very difficult, as a young teenager, giving out tracts on the beach and coming across an old tramp. To me it seemed so cold and unfeeling to push a piece of paper into his hungry hands; it would make a mockery of the very words of life. What can we do? I certainly felt very helpless. Much to the disgust of my friends, I would give him money – which, they told me, probably rightly, he would spend on alcohol. In my heart I felt that if that brought him a moment's pleasure I was glad, but the cracks in the walls were widening. It's difficult at times to see beyond the masks that people wear to the basic hungry human underneath.

I remember one day walking down the King's Road in London and being stopped by a filthy old man who asked for money. I suggested to him that we went for something to eat together and he agreed. After some time of embarrassed silence, we began to talk a little. To my surprise, I discovered that he was a very intelligent man who had been a doctor. He was an alcoholic and, by that destructive decaying existence, he had lost everything that he once valued – his wife, his children, his home. It was such a lesson to me, although I'm sure I'll never really learn it, to look beyond outward appearances.

Just a few months ago we were doing a concert in Florida.

I left the theatre for a while in the afternoon to get some fresh air. Coming back again, I was faced by a very pathetic, emaciated man, bare from the waist up. He frightened me by the way he grabbed my arm and the wild stare in his eyes. I had a cup of coffee in my hand that I'd got 'to go' from a restaurant. He told me that he was cold and thirsty. I quickly gave him my coffee and rushed off, with my heart thumping. Later that evening, when the concert was over, I was talking to some kids outside the front of the theatre. I suddenly saw the man come out of the theatre with a T-shirt on and walk away. I found the people who were selling the T-shirts and asked them about him. They told me that some kids had seen him outside, bought him a ticket and a shirt, and taken him in. Love in action – practical, caring Christianity. This surely is the heart of the gospel. You only need to read a few verses in the books of Hosea and Amos to understand how caring and just and socially concerned our Father God really is.

'Hear the word of the Lord, O people of Israel; for the Lord has a controversy with the inhabitants of the land. There is no faithfulness or kindness, and no knowledge of God in the land; there is swearing, lying, killing, stealing, and committing adultery . . . Therefore the land mourns' (Hosea 4:1–3).

When Jesus was fulfilling His three-year ministry on earth, He too showed practical loving provision. He wept with Mary and Martha over the death of their brother. When the crowds gathered on the mountainside to hear Him speak, He fed them. He could so easily have ignored these mundane practical preparations, but He chose to supply them.

When I look at our modern world and at the Church, I wonder at times how we have managed to stray from the heart of the message. Jesus spent His time with the common people, with the socially unacceptable. How are we as Christians to meet the groaning needs of the Third World, of those who die in their masses every day? People like Mother Teresa, who lives among the poor on the streets of Calcutta in India, show us how.

When I was very little, I hated green vegetables, especially Brussels sprouts. My mum would try and encourage me to eat a few, telling me to think of the starving millions. I simply told her I would be very happy for her to send my sprouts to them. The trouble with TV coverage of the disastrous world condition is that in time we become immune. We are so used to watching fantasy and make-believe horror on the box that we have learned ways of switching off from the real things. Probably many of you wonder what is the point of watching; it only greatly upsets you and you are powerless to help. That's not true. We can make a difference. Organisations like Tear Fund in Britain, and Compassion and World Vision in America make it possible for you and me to reach across the world.

I work a lot with Compassion on my US tours and their slogan is that one man can't change the world, but you can change the world for one man! They have developed a scheme whereby I can present their case in concert. They provide me, at the beginning of each tour, with leaflets explaining their work, with a tear-off portion. In just a few moments of concert time, I try to explain to people the whole idea behind child sponsorship. People are encouraged to take on one little boy or girl as their own love project and, by a very reasonable monthly sum, provide basic food, clothing and education for them. You are also able to write to the child and they will reply and send you some information about their life and family.

You may say that this is just a drop in the bucket, but you tell that to the child who's been given a chance to live! The world stood and applauded when Bob Geldof and all the other musicians presented Live Aid – and rightly so. Organisations like the ones I've mentioned have been there for years, working away to alleviate pain. Pray for them.

Become involved. Every person who says 'yes' affects one more life.

The two little girls we sponsor live in India. Seven hundred and twenty million people live in that vast country, where eighty-three per cent of the population are Hindu. The children, Shanthi and Shiny, write to us and tell us all about their Sunday school lessons and what they have learned about Jesus. We treasure their letters.

One of the most exciting new projects to be undertaken by Youth For Christ in the last few years has been their scheme to help the unemployed in our land. Many kids leaving school today know that they will never work. Many students qualifying from university know that they will not be able to find a job within their profession. Work is totally basic and essential to man and his dignity. In our culture, a man who has had the right to work taken away from him feels worthless and degraded.

Not so long ago, I bumped into a boy who had been in my brother's class at school. I couldn't believe the change in him. We chatted for a while and he told me that he hadn't really had a job in seven years. From being a fairly smart person, he now looked dirty, long-haired and aimless.

I'm sure that much of the violence we see in the streets and in football crowds is largely caused by these kinds of problem. When you rob someone of their self worth, they lose their self-respect, and very soon their respect for others. Youth For Christ began making a register of the unemployed in the areas where they work, and actively sought ways of employing them. As Christians, we cannot think that these people are not our concern. Jesus died for them and it's our privilege and responsibility to try and act on behalf of the millions who wonder who they are.

I am not a very knowledgeable person politically. I've never really studied any party manifesto. My concern is for the things that hang over our world that cause alarm to the man in the street. One of those issues is nuclear war. The

American dramatisation *The Day After* and the British production *Threads* had a very severe and sobering effect on much of our community. If you are an atheist or agnostic, having no belief in an after-life, the thought of having humanity wiped out in moments must be the ultimate madness. Some have said that, if you don't believe in anything, why hang on any longer? Why worry if we are all destroyed? It will happen sooner or later. Issues are never that black and white. Many people would not claim to believe in God, but are groping to believe in something, and the thought of the horror of a nuclear winter is a desperate one.

I recorded a song on my 'Don't Hide Your Heart' album called 'Under The Gun'. The last line of the chorus is: 'But there's one place to run, run to the Son.' The song was actually written for Cliff by two American writers who weren't Christians. Cliff changed the lyrics a little. They had originally written: 'But there's nowhere to run under the gun.' We know that there is a future and a hope. We may not be spared some of the pain, but we know whose hands we are really in.

How can we keep such a message of hope to ourselves? There are so many cases that cry out for hope. Terminal illnesses, such as cancer, and the rapidly increasing disease of AIDS, are rife among us. People struggle to maintain a semblance of dignity in the face of death. As God's people we can look at illnesses like AIDS and clearly see God's punishment on a sick world, but let us never forget though that, although Jesus hates sin, He always loves the sinner.

Steve Taylor tells a very moving story about a young girl in Washington DC who has made it her ministry to visit dying AIDS patients. She takes them flowers and biscuits, chats to them, reads to them. When they ask her why, knowing that they are shunned by others, she tells them about a man who touched lepers. Several of these men have repented and given their lives to God before they've died.

Sometimes we find it easier to hate the sin than to love the sinner.

One of the places I always find fascinating to visit is Las Vegas. From the moment you step off the aeroplane in the little desert town, you are confronted with fruit machines of every conceivable variety. We work with Calvary Chapel there, doing concerts, and they always accommodate us in one of the huge hotels on the Strip. The reception area is actually a large casino. I stood beside a man one day and watched him lose $10,000 in a very short time. People stay up and gamble all night, convinced that this will be the night their luck changes. The first time we were there, as we went to bed, I spotted an old lady of about eighty, sitting on a stool with a huge bucket of money, feeding it into a hungry machine. When Norman and I came down for breakfast the next morning, she was still there, at the same machine! We went back again the next year for a summer concert. After the evening, a mother came up to me to thank me. She told me that her daughter had come out of hospital that day for three hours to come to the concert; she had tried to take her own life. No matter what you may think of suicide or the legal ramifications, the torture in a human soul to make that the only viable option is a horrific thought. Horrific it may be, but very common it is certainly becoming. All across America and, to a lesser degree, in the UK, teenagers are choosing to end their lives, many of them successfully. If your parents, your conscience, your peer group, your entertainment, are all shouting opposing ideas in your head, who do you listen to? Where are the absolutes? God's Word tells us the value that is placed on a human life. The greatest price of all is the death of the Lord Jesus. It would be great if some of our churches could set up counselling facilities for kids in real need, with a 'hot line' for when it gets too much to bear. 'Blessed are the peacemakers, for they shall be called sons of God' (Matthew 5:9).

It was a quiet Monday morning and I was waiting for a

tube at Oxford Circus Station in London. As it pulled in and
the doors opened, I went to enter and was knocked on to
the platform by two young boys. I don't think they could
have been any older than twelve or thirteen. I couldn't
work out what was wrong with them, as they seemed
totally disorientated, until I saw the crisp bags in their
hands. Glue-sniffing is ruining the health of many young
kids who simply don't know what to be doing with themselves. Drug abuse and teenage alcoholism are at an all-
time high in our nation. There are few more pathetic sights
than seeing youngsters totally out of control, with no idea
where or who they are. These ills never travel alone. With
many girls, drug addictions and prostitution come hand in
hand. They are charged very little by pushers until they are
hooked, and then the prices go sky-high. The only avenues
open to them are to sell their bodies to raise cash to support
their 'habit'. Most of the men higher on the drug racket
ladder are raking in money at the expense of young lives.

The last time I crossed the border from Switzerland into
Germany, we were all taken out of our bus and searched
carefully. We were lined up and sniffer dogs were taken
past us. Only that morning, I was told later, they had
recovered several ounces of cocaine heading for the city
streets.

> Sipping whisky from a paper cup,
> you drown your sorrows till you can't stand up,
> why don't you look into Jesus –
> He's got the answer.
>
> *(Larry Norman)*

Our prisons are crammed to overflowing with the products of a violent age and the condition of man's heart.
Many young people who get involved in crime at a very
basic, fairly harmless level return from our Borstals and
juvenile detention centres hardened and embittered.

Homosexual rape is rampant. Violence within prisons is accelerated by overcrowding.

I watched the two movies made about boys' and girls' Borstals – *Scum* and *Scrubbers*. They were shocking but, I know, an accurate portrayal of life as it is lived behind the walls of our penitentiaries.

It would probably surprise you how receptive prisoners are to outside visits. I find that, especially in the top security prisons, they are so grateful to people from the 'free world' for coming in. Jesus said, 'I was sick and you never came to visit me, I was hungry and you gave me no food, I was cold and you gave me nothing to wear, I was in prison and you never came to see me.' When Jesus said that if we do this to the least and lowliest person we do it to Him, I have a feeling He meant it much more literally than we take it.

Sometimes we take the sayings and words of Jesus and over-spiritualise them, when we were actually meant to take them as they were written. There are so many situations that cry out for our help and input as God's people. One-parent families, sexually abused children, the aged, homosexuals, the sick and dying, widows, orphans – the list is endless. We cannot all take up every standard, and try and pioneer every cause, but let's ask the Lord what we can do to be His hands, feet and heart in our world.

Is a rich man worth more than a poor man?
Is a stranger worth less than a friend?
Is a baby worth more than an old man?
Your beginning worth more than your end?

If you heard that your life had been valued,
that the price had been paid on the nail,
would you ask what was traded,
how much and who paid it,
who was he and what was his name?

If you heard that his name was called Jesus,
would you say that the price was too dear?
Held to the cross, not by nails but by love,
it was you broke his heart, not the spear.

Would you say you are worth what it cost him?
You say no, but the price stays the same.
If it don't make you easy,
Laugh it off, pass him by,
but remember the day when you throw it away
that he paid what he thought you were worth.

(Graham Kendrick)

13

TRIUMPH IN THE AIR

When Steve Taylor and I toured Great Britain in 1985, it was so exciting to have a lot of people who didn't know God at all coming to the concerts because of the TV show. Many told me how they had given their lives to God in their own homes, through what someone shared or sang. God is raising up all sorts of singers and musicians to proclaim the ways of His kingdom. One of these people is undoubtedly Steve Taylor. He and his wife, Debbie, are very creative, talented people. I admire his honesty, his humour, his insight and his taste in women!

David Pawson once said that music is either prophetic or nostalgic. I pray that God will grant us musicians in this country who will sing out songs from the Father's heart.

I don't think that there has ever been a time when it's been more exciting to be a Christian. Some time ago in Cobham we felt as if the Lord was saying to us, as a church, that the moment had come to change our role. For a while we had played the part of a holiday ship, inviting people on to rest and have a good time. We feel that God is telling us now that it is time to be a battleship. We cannot rush heedlessly at the enemy lines unprepared and armourless, but by His grace we will put on our 'spiritual armour' and together go forward as an army of love and light to do battle in Jesus' name. The world is watching and waiting.

Within the kingdom there is work for us all to do. One of the things that is most unhealthy about full-time Christian work is that often we end up knowing that God can use those whom we look up to, but what about us? If you look at the kind of men that the Lord chose, that should in many ways be an encouragement to us all. God is not a talent scout; He is looking for obedient loving hearts. It doesn't matter if you are ten years old or eighty; if your heart is after God, then He will use you. There are many things that we know to be true because we read them in God's Word, but in reality they are hard to absorb. It's impossible to comprehend that the same God who raised Jesus from the dead lives in our hearts by the Holy Spirit, but it's true. If you study the lives of many of the best-known men and women of God, you'll be amazed at their normality. When the Lord swept the face of the earth looking for a man to use, He wasn't looking for a Master's Degree, but simply a heart that said, 'Send me.'

For many of us, we find our place in God's kingdom at home, serving Him through our local fellowships, but others have a different call. Many young people have a desire to travel overseas and work, either long- or short-term, with various societies. I think it's wonderful for us to move out of what we know and are secure with, and see something of God's world. Organisations like Operation Mobilisation and Youth With A Mission take on young people for varying lengths of time. One of the marvellous aspects of their set-up is the practical training in evangelism that they will give you 'on the job'. I have tremendous respect for OM, and their leader, George Verwer, in particular. He is a man full of zeal and commitment to spreading the gospel worldwide. YWAM run discipleship training schools which last for about three months at a time. They even have one on Hawaii, where you could suffer for the Lord on the beaches!

I'm thirty years old this year. As I look back over the life I've lived so far, I feel I can see more clearly now the way that the Lord has directed me. Sometimes I've been very aware of what was the right thing to do, and at other times there has been no 'writing on the wall'. I really believe though that, if our lives are committed to Him, and the desire of our hearts is to please God and serve our fellow man, God will make the pathway clear. I'm sure too that God is big enough to handle our mistakes. I used to be so afraid of doing anything, in case I got it wrong. God wants us to be secure in His love. His will is not like a tightrope where we balance precariously, knowing that the slightest wind could blow us off. I've got many things wrong in my life. I'm rushed into things inadvisedly at times, but God's love and grace have always been with me. He is committed to His people.

It's sad sometimes when I look back at friends who I had so much fun with. We've shared such a lot about the Lord together, and now they've walked away from it all. Why is it that, when we are a bit older and more respectable, so often our love and fervour for God seems to die away?

In Jeremiah 2:11 the Lord's complaint was: 'Has a nation changed its gods, even though they are no gods? But my people have changed their glory for that which does not profit.' It would seem totally inconceivable that the nations who worshipped pieces of wood and rock stood loyally by them, while the people of the living God went shopping. Nothing has really changed.

To my mind there can be no more miserable existence than that of the 'one day a week' believer. Having one foot on either side of the fence is a most uncomfortable position! You don't enjoy God's presence fully because you're not walking with Him, but neither can you totally throw off all influence of Christianity and enjoy flying in the face of what you know to be right. Why should it be that, while Jehovah's Witnesses, Mormons and Buddhists hang in there, many of us as evangelical Christians come and go? Has it to do with the fact that God asks for our hearts? We are given choice, freedom, but it is also required that we

lay everything we have and are on the altar. In reality
there is no middle ground; we are either for Him or against
Him. As Elijah put it to the false prophets of Baal: 'How
long will you halt between two opinions? Choose today
who really is God.'

We could have been created as programmed robots who
automatically loved and served our Creator. God wanted
more than that; He wants to be our friend. He wants us to
choose to love Him. In Jeremiah 2:19, He says that the
reasons our hearts are so faithless is because we are not in
awe of God. I'm sure that is true today. The miracle of the
gospel is that the very one who created the whole universe,
who holds all the planets in place, should die for me, to give
me a chance to be where He is. The book of Hebrews
proclaims the radical news that, because of what Christ did
on the cross, we can enter the very throne room of heaven
and cry, 'Abba, Father' – literally 'Daddy'. How do we hold
the two in tension – familiarity and majesty, accessibility
and holiness? We know that He's our Father; we talk to Him
about our daily lives. But round the throne constantly
angels hide their faces and cry, 'Holy!' We come boldly into
His presence because of the blood of Jesus, and yet His
ways and thoughts are higher than ours in every sense.

Perhaps so often we fall away because our own hearts
condemn us, and we feel that we have failed. If only I could
encourage you, make you see how special you are to the
living God. Some of you feel that you have made too many
mistakes. That's not true – forgiveness is here for us all.
Some of you feel as if you have nothing to give: God has so
much that He wants to put in your hands.

Just recently I flew over to Holland to take part in a youth
event sponsored by a television company. They had 22,000
kids gathered from all over the country. The other singer
with me was a girl called Joni; I'm sure many of you will be
aware of who she is. She was a very energetic, lively,
sport-orientated girl, who broke her neck in a diving acci-

dent. Confined to a wheelchair for life, she struggled with why God had allowed this to happen to her. As we sat on stage together, singing 'Seek ye first the kingdom of God and His righteousness, and all these things shall be added unto you', I had to marvel at our God. There is no god like the living God. He can take a broken bruised life and fill it with the power of His love and His Spirit and touch the lives of millions of people through her.

I can't believe how many basic mistakes I still make. Recently I received quite a lesson on judging by appearances! A youth pastor had asked me to do a concert in a very little church. He warned me that there would only be about fifty people, but he was very keen that we should go. It had been a long tiring week and I was a bit fed up by the time we arrived. The stage was so small that I didn't dare put a glass of water out, as I knew that I'd end up swimming in it! We went out to begin singing and couldn't believe where the audience were sitting. Forty-nine of them were in the back row! Right in the front, in a bright orange T-shirt sat one little man. After each song, the back row would clap and the man at the front would just sit and smile at us. I began to get mad. I thought, 'If he doesn't like us, if he doesn't want to clap at all, I'm sure they could have squeezed one more in at the back!' We finished the first half and I sat in the dressing-room, feeling sorry for myself and moaning to the band about this one man. Just then there was a funny banging noise at the door. I opened it and was face to face with the man in the luminous T-shirt. 'I've just come to say how much I'm enjoying the concert. I love your music and pray for you every day.' As I looked down at this little man, I saw that he had no arms. I cannot begin to tell you what a total jerk I felt. When will I ever learn?

As I look to the future, I'm really excited about so many things. I shall be spending a month in India soon; I've always felt that one day I would go there. When I was at

London Bible College, I bought a map of India and had it up on my wall for two years. I used to pray for the country and its people, and feel such a burden for them. Many days I would just weep as I looked at that huge area of land and felt something of the terrible need and suffering. Norman and I hope to visit our two little girls and take a film crew over to do a documentary of life in India and the work of the relief organisations that work there.

I received a letter from a senator's wife in Washington recently. In America they have a programme called *The 700 Club*. I had been asked to appear on the show and be interviewed. Norman and I flew into Virginia Beach and stayed in a hotel that night, preparing for the next morning's programme. We arrived at the studio and met the other people on the show that day. One gentleman was a news correspondent who had been held hostage in Beirut for eleven months, chained to a radiator. He had eventually escaped and was now reunited with his wife. It was riveting to listen to him and to feel the burden that was on his heart for his fellow Americans still being held. I felt that my contribution seemed frivolous by comparison. After the show we went out to lunch together and he told me how excited he and his wife were about what I'd said. I was amazed! They told me that many of the politicians and their wives in Washington were very concerned about the whole rock music world. Lyrics in songs have become very overt, with strong sexual, Satanic and violent overtones. They asked me if I would like to work with them in trying to clean up the business and offer an alternative to kids who are looking for something to get excited about. I said yes!

Surely we live in a most challenging time, when the world is being held hostage by greed and hate. Those of us who have been bought back have so much to say. Of all the songs I'll ever sing, none has captivated my heart and mind more than Graham Kendrick's *Fighter*. I can think of no better words to leave you with.

Fighter

My eyes may see the coming King in all His majesty
In company all dressed in white,
But meanwhile here at the world's dark end
The nations see no future, waiting for the serpent to
    strike.
And souls grow weary in this war of love
And seek their solace strolling down the sweet civilian
    ways,
But meanwhile back at the world's dark end
The dragon draws the iron curtain round against the
    light.
  Where have all the Christian soldiers gone?
  Where is the resistance, will no-one be strong?
  When will we stand up tall and straight,
  Rise up and storm the gate?
  How can we fail to be excited?
  The battle is ours, why don't we fight it?
  Battalions of darkness rise above me,
  But God put a fighter in me, a fighter in me.
  So we will sing songs of victory,
  We will arise and set men free,
  We will applaud your majesty,
  We will proclaim your kingdom come,
  We will announce the battle done,
  We will lift up the Righteous One.

(Graham Kendrick)